Kwoklyn Wan

SIMPLE, MODERN RECIPES
FOR EVERY DAY

CHINESE MADE EASY

cover illustration by Jordan Amy Lee
photography by Sam Folan

quadrille

INTRODUCTION

Delving into the world of Chinese cuisine is akin to embarking on an epic journey, one that traverses vast landscapes, rich histories and diverse cultures. Chinese food has a millennia-old legacy, and has evolved alongside many East Asian cuisines. From the delicate sushi rolls of Japan and the spicy ferments of Korea, to the aromatic broths of Indonesia, the echoes of Chinese culinary traditions resonate throughout East Asia. This is a testament to China's profound culinary influence and the universal appeal of its flavours and techniques.

Yet, while the depth and complexity of Chinese cuisine are celebrated, it's often perceived as intricate and demanding. In this book, I want to challenge that belief. My aim is to make the essence of Chinese cooking accessible and enjoyable for every home cook, wherever in the world you may be.

China's vastness, both geographically and culturally, has birthed an incredible variety in its culinary repertoire. From the fiery heat of Sichuan's peppercorns to the subtle, delicate steamed dishes of the coastal regions; from the hearty, wheat-based dishes of the north to the rice-centric meals of the south – the country's cuisine is a tapestry of regional specialties. These dishes and techniques, in their various forms, have traversed borders, and this has, in turn, influenced the food cultures of neighbouring East Asian nations.

However, if we peel back the layers of history and geography, we find core principles and techniques that form the backbone of Chinese cooking. At its heart, Chinese cooking is about simplicity, balance and harmony. A dish may balance the crunchiness of a deep-fried morsel with the softness of steamed rice or combine the freshness of vegetables with the depth of a fermented sauce. This dance of contrasts and complements is intrinsic to its nature.

The wok stands as a symbol of this culinary dance. It's not just a cooking vessel but an instrument of creativity and versatility. With its deep, concave shape, the wok invites a range of techniques, from high-heat stir-frying to gentle steaming. Its efficiency and adaptability have made it an enduring fixture of Chinese kitchens and, by extension, of many East Asian cooking traditions.

This book embraces this culinary legacy, simplifying recipes without sacrificing their heart and soul. My aim is to prove that with a few essential tools, staple ingredients and a dash of passion, the magic of Chinese dishes is well within reach.

Moreover, the spirit of Chinese cooking lies in improvisation and adaptability. As seen in its influence across East Asia, Chinese cuisine has an innate ability to evolve, assimilate and resonate. This book encourages you to embrace that spirit, to adjust and experiment based on your tastes, ensuring each dish becomes a reflection of your unique touch.

So, as you turn these pages, you're not just exploring recipes; you're delving into a rich tapestry of culinary narratives, technique and histories. Here's to a journey that promises both simplicity and discovery.

Welcome to *Chinese Made Easy.*

THE ART OF PREPARATION

The art of preparation is the foundation of traditional Chinese and East Asian cooking, and a reminder of the age-old adage: 'Well-begun is half-done.' This prep-centric approach is favoured by these cuisines because it allows the cooking process to flow seamlessly, making it easy to create flavourful, aesthetically pleasing food.

Preparing ingredients beforehand, also known as *mise en place* (French for 'everything in its place'), is especially important for the quick cooking methods used in Chinese and East Asian cooking. When swiftly stir-frying in a wok, for instance, there is little room for last-minute chopping – and attempting to do so, no matter how valiantly, will likely hamper your enjoyment both in the kitchen and at the table. For the harmonious layering of flavours and textures that's ubiquitous in Chinese cuisine, each ingredient needs to be ready to be tossed into the pan at precisely the right moment.

Pre-preparing elements of your dish simplifies the hands-on cooking part of the process. It also enhances the quality, taste and texture of the final product. Take battered chicken or beef: pre-frying these ingredients is common practice in Chinese cuisine. This not only reduces the cooking time later, but it also locks in flavour and transforms the texture. A quick re-fry during the final cooking phase is more than a way of reheating the meat: it also elevates the crispiness, giving you that delicious juxtaposition of crunchy batter against silky-smooth sauce. These methods are invaluable, especially when you are cooking multiple dishes at once, as they streamline the process and make complex recipes that much more manageable. The best part is that they don't compromise on taste: they improve it.

The philosophy of Chinese and East Asian cuisine is, in a word, balance. By preparing ingredients and pre-cooking certain elements of your dishes, your food can embody this philosophy: there is both preparation and spontaneity, layering of flavours, and the immediate pleasure of good food made with foresight and skill.

INGREDIENTS

Cloves
Cloves are a prized spice in Chinese cooking, cherished for their intense aroma and a spicy sweetness, adding depth to slow-cooked stews and braised meats and enhancing complex flavours.

Star anise
Star anise is, as the name suggests, a star-shaped spice that brings a warm, liquorice-like flavour to Chinese dishes. It's a key ingredient in the classic five-spice powder.

Cinnamon
Cinnamon infuses a comforting depth and complexity into braises and soups. Use ground or sticks as the recipe calls for.

Chinese rice wine
Chinese rice wine, or Shaoxing wine, is made from fermented rice and brings a rich, savoury depth to dishes. Slightly sweet and nutty, with a pungent aroma, it's commonly used in sauces, to tenderize meat or to caramelize stir-fries.

Cornflour (cornstarch)
Cornflour is primarily used as a thickening agent, giving a glossy finish and a silky-smooth texture. It is also crucial in the technique of velveting (see page 25).

Spring onions (scallions)
Spring onions are part of the 'holy trinity' of Cantonese cooking, which also encompasses ginger and garlic. Chinese kitchens use the whole onion – white for earthiness, green for freshness – not just one end like in Western kitchens.

Fermented black beans
Known as douchi in Mandarin, these are not black beans but small, dried soybeans that have been fermented with salt and spices. Intensely aromatic, douchi are used to enhance meat dishes, stir-fries, and sauces while providing a unique, pungent umami depth.

Ginger
Ginger is used both for its flavour and purported health benefits. It lifts stir-fries, soups and teas, and is said to aid digestion and relieve nausea in Traditional Chinese Medicine.

Chinese black vinegar

Chinese black vinegar is known for its robust, smoky flavour. Made from fermented rice (sorghum), it is both tart and sweet, with a deep umami finish. It's used as a dipping sauce for dumplings.

Chillies

In Chinese cuisine, chillies come in many forms and are used not just for their heat but for their colour and aroma, too. Bold and spicy flavours are especially prevalent in regions like Sichuan (where Sichuan peppercorns originate) and Hunan.

Water chestnuts

Known for their crisp texture and slightly sweet, nutty flavour, these aquatic vegetables are used fresh or canned to add texture to everything from stir-fries and dumplings to salads and soups.

Chinese five spice

This spice blend combines star anise, cloves, Chinese cinnamon, Sichuan pepper and fennel seeds, tapping into the five core flavours: sweet, sour, salty, bitter and umami. It is widely used to marinate meats, season stews and even to elevate sweet dishes.

Tofu

This Chinese staple is high in protein and vegetarian, and it absorbs flavours beautifully. Look for soft tofu for soups and desserts, or firm tofu if you are stir-frying, deep-frying or grilling.

Sesame seeds, oil and paste

Sesame is integral to Chinese cooking. Toasted sesame seeds are often sprinkled over stir-fries, salads and noodles for added texture and taste, while sesame oil is used for frying and brings a deep, rich flavour to dishes.

Bean sprouts

Bean sprouts come from mung beans and are favourites in stir-fries, spring rolls and salads. These are typically added towards the end of the cooking process to maintain their crispness.

Honey

Runny honey is commonly used in glazes, marinades and for caramelization. Use a mild honey for sweetness that doesn't overpower. It may even bring you health benefits, too.

CONDIMENTS

Light soy sauce

Light soy sauce is a clear, amber-hued condiment brewed from soybeans, wheat, salt and water. Beyond its characteristic saltiness, it imparts umami and a touch of sweetness to dishes, making it ideal for seasoning and marinating. Its unique flavour is a result of the fermentation process.

Light soy sauce contains gluten thanks to the wheat. If you're sensitive to gluten, light soy sauce can be substituted with tamari, a Japanese condiment. Tamari is traditionally wheat-free but offers a similar umami depth, albeit with a slightly thicker texture and less sharp taste. When replacing light soy sauce with tamari, taste as you go: you will likely need to adjust the quantities to balance the flavours within your dish.

Dark soy sauce

Dark soy sauce is a Chinese and East Asian culinary essential. Thicker than its light counterpart, dark soy sauce is fermented for longer and often has added molasses or caramel, which grant it a richer, sweeter taste and a dense, almost syrupy consistency. It's not just a seasoning agent but a colourant, giving dishes their signature deep brown hue. The robust flavour and colour of dark soy sauce make it ideal for braised dishes, marinades and glazes, where its full-bodied taste shines through.

If you don't have dark soy sauce to hand, you can mix a light soy sauce with a touch of brown sugar or molasses in a pinch. This will imitate the sweetness and depth of dark soy sauce, though it won't be a perfect match – always adjust to taste, ensuring the balance is right for your dish.

Oyster sauce

Oyster sauce is a lustrous, thick condiment widely used in Chinese cuisine and other East Asian and Southeast Asian dishes. Originally made from just oyster juices, salt and sugar, modern oyster sauce often incorporates soy sauce and other flavour enhancers. Its rich, umami-packed profile brings depth to dishes, adding both sweetness and saltiness in just the right proportions.

OYSTER SAUCE
PRODUCT OF THAILAND
Allergy Advice
For allergens,
IMPORTED BY
PRODUCT OF THAILAND
同珍
甜
醋
Sweetened
Rice

Predominantly used in stir-fries, marinades and to finish dishes, oyster sauce enhances everything from vegetables to meats, making it a pantry essential for lovers of Chinese cuisine.

Oyster sauce is available at bigger and Asian supermarkets, but if you need to substitute it, combine light soy sauce with a touch of hoisin sauce. This will provide a balance of sweet and salty flavours and, while it doesn't replicate the distinct oyster essence, it delivers the depth and richness that oyster sauce is known for. Adjust the mix to taste, ensuring your dish retains its balance and desired flavours.

Hoisin sauce

Sweet, tangy and umami-rich, hoisin sauce is made from a blend of soybeans, sugar, vinegar and a mix of spices. It has an almost jam-like consistency, making it ideal for use in marinades and dipping sauces.

Hoisin is best known for its use in Peking duck and moo shu pork, where it lends a distinct sweetness, but with savoury undertones. It can also be used to elevate stir-fries, or even for a non-traditional take on Vietnamese bánh mì.

To substitute hoisin sauce, mix together soy sauce (for saltiness), peanut butter or black bean paste (for umami), a dash of vinegar (for tanginess) and honey or brown sugar (for sweetness). Adjust the ingredients to taste: it won't be exactly the same as a traditional, complex hoisin sauce, but it will still bring a touch of sweetness and tanginess.

Doubanjiang

Also known as spicy fermented bean paste, doubanjiang is an essential ingredient in many Sichuan dishes including mapo tofu and twice-cooked pork. Made from a mixture of fermented broad beans, soybeans, salt, rice and various spices, including red chilli paste, this piquant paste packs an umami punch.

Doubanjiang is so unique that substituting it can be a challenge. In a pinch, a mix of black bean paste or sauce mixed with a hot chilli paste or sriracha will provide a similar level of heat and umami. Always tweak the proportions according to your own tastes: if you like it less spicy, add less chilli. If you're a fiend for fiery flavours, go all in.

Sesame oil

Known for its intense and nutty aroma and flavour, this amber-hued oil is extracted from toasted sesame seeds. It's well-loved and frequently used in East and Southeast Asian dishes, either for stir-frying or for drizzling onto dishes, where it releases a distinctively warm and rich scent.

Chicken powder

Chicken powder, often found in the form of bouillon cubes or granules, is a concentrated seasoning that imparts a rich, poultry-flavoured essence to dishes. Derived from chicken broth, it then undergoes a dehydration process which makes it both convenient and shelf-stable.

This powder is frequently used in soups, stews, sauces and even stir-fries to heighten the savoury, umami undertones and add depth to the overall flavour. However, it often contains high amounts of salt, MSG and other flavourings, and is obviously non-vegetarian, so you can use the following alternatives, if you wish:

Vegetable bouillon – While this won't give the distinct poultry taste that chicken powder brings to a dish, it can offer a rich umami profile that is vegetarian-friendly.

Homemade seasoning blend – A mixture of basic seasonings can emulate chicken powder. Start with a tablespoon each of paprika, Chinese five spice, garlic powder and onion powder and 3 tablespoons of celery salt, then season with salt and white pepper and adjust to taste as needed. You can add a touch of ground turmeric for colour, too, if you like.

Fish sauce

Fish sauce, derived from fermented fish and salt, is a Southeast Asian staple known for its pungent aroma and umami depth. Commonly used in Thai and Vietnamese cuisines, its distinct flavour is unparalleled.

If you don't have fish sauce, or you need your dish to be vegetarian, try one of the following:

Soy sauce – Offers saltiness and umami, albeit without the brininess of fish sauce. Fish sauce is typically saltier, with a more concentrated flavour than soy sauce, so you'll need to adjust your quantities accordingly. As always, taste as you go.

Tamari – A deeper, gluten-free version of soy sauce that hails from Japan (see page 12). As for Chinese soy sauce, you'll want to adjust the quantities slightly for maximum flavour.

Vegan fish sauce – A blend of seaweed, mushrooms and soy, vegan fish sauce is available at bigger supermarkets and health food shops. It brings a similar saltiness without relying on anchovies for flavour and can be substituted 1:1.

Homemade blend – For an alternative take on the flavour of fish sauce, try mixing soy sauce with seaweed broth for a citrussy tang.

NOODLES, RICE AND WRAPPERS

Dried vs. ready-to-wok noodles

Noodles are a staple in many East Asian dishes, and choosing between dried and ready-to-wok varieties will influence your dish. Dried noodles offer springiness and elasticity with satisfying bite, and are commonly used in traditional dishes.

Ready-to-wok noodles are perfect for quick meals as they can be tossed directly into your stir-fry or soup. The texture is not as springy as traditional dried noodles, but both achieve a similar flavour.

Thai fragrant rice

Also known as Hom Mali rice, Thai fragrant rice is known for its distinctive jasmine scent and slightly sticky texture when cooked. It is a long-grain variety that becomes fluffy and slightly clingy, making it perfect for soaking up the flavours of curries and sauces.

Jasmine rice

Similar to Thai fragrant rice but grown primarily in Thailand and Cambodia, jasmine rice is prized for its rich aromatic scent and subtly sweet flavour. It has a soft and slightly sticky texture after cooking.

Glutinous rice

Often referred to as sticky rice, this type of rice becomes glue-like when cooked, and is essential in many Asian dishes, both savoury and sweet, such as Chinese zongzi (rice dumplings) or Thai mango sticky rice.

Sushi rice

A variety of short-grain rice known as Japonica, sushi rice is characterized by its ability to clump together, making it essential for sushi rolls. It is usually seasoned with a mix of vinegar, sugar and salt.

Wrappers

Wonton skins – These are thin, square sheets of dough made from flour, egg, water and salt. Wontons can encase a variety of fillings and, once filled, they can be boiled, steamed or fried, for use in dishes like wonton soup or crispy fried wontons.

Pancake roll wrappers – Also known as spring roll wrappers, these are typically larger and slightly thicker than wonton skins and are used to make spring rolls. Made from a mixture of flour and water, these wrappers become crisp and golden when fried, for that characteristic crunchy exterior.

Rice paper wrappers – Made from rice flour and water, these wrappers are thin, translucent and pliable when moistened. They are commonly used in Vietnamese cuisine for dishes like summer rolls, where they are filled with shrimp, fresh herbs, lettuce and vermicelli noodles. Rice paper wrappers are eaten fresh and do not require cooking.

All the rice varieties and wrappers can be found in most major supermarkets.

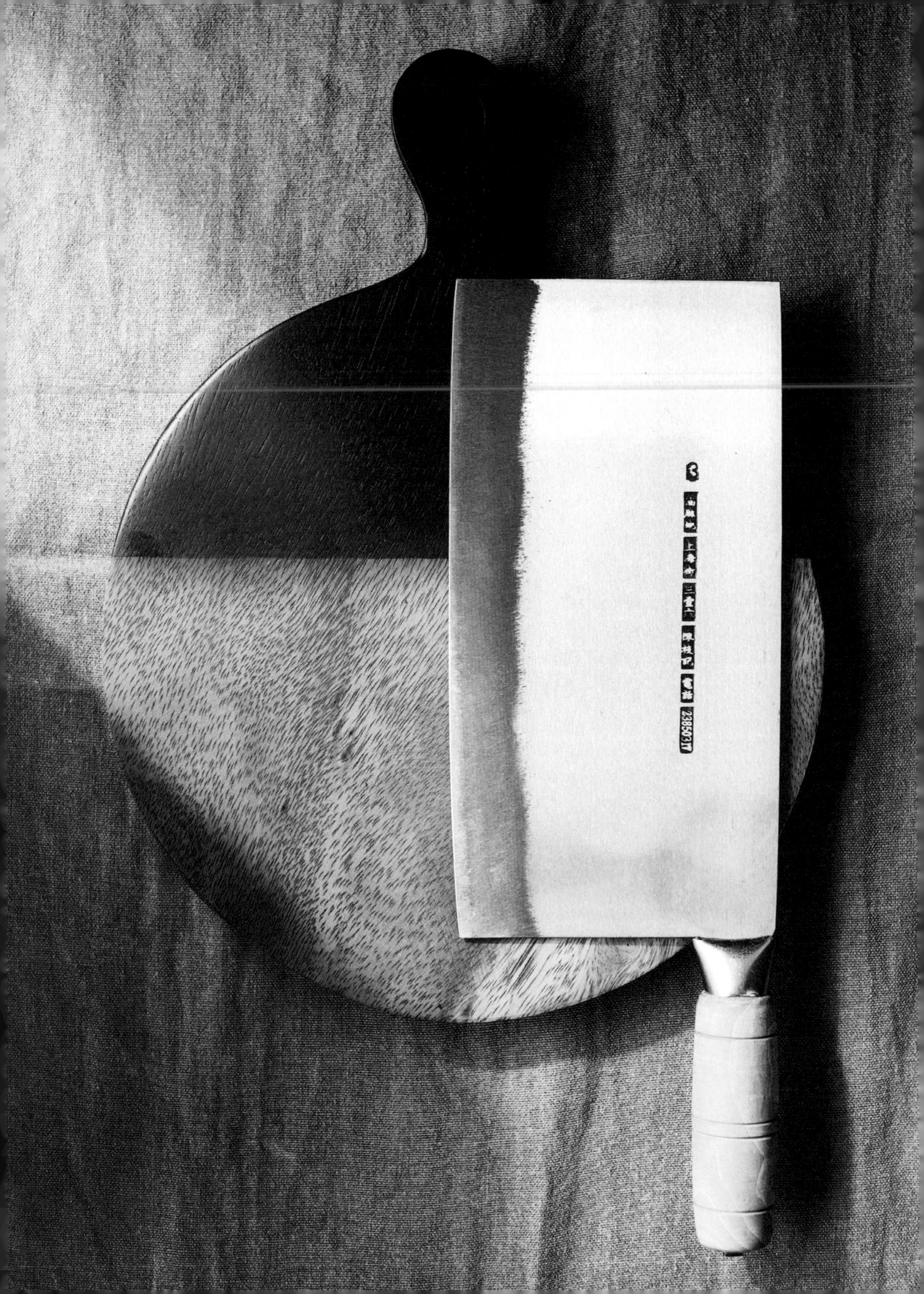

USEFUL EQUIPMENT

The wok

The wok, with its distinctive round-bottomed shape, is a cornerstone of Chinese and East Asian cooking, perfect for everything from stir-frying to deep-frying, steaming or braising. When it comes to choosing the right wok, the debate often centres around two popular materials: carbon steel and non-stick.

Carbon steel

- Heat responsiveness – Carbon steel woks heat up and cool down rapidly, providing chefs with precise temperature control. This makes them ideal for the quick, high-heat cooking methods typical in Chinese and other East Asian cuisines.

- Durability – With proper care, a carbon steel wok can last a lifetime. It also gets better with age: repeated use seasons the wok, enhancing its natural non-stick properties.

- Authentic taste – Many chefs believe that carbon steel woks impart wok hei or 'breath of the wok' – the distinct smokiness produced by stir-frying at high temperatures – into your food.

Non-stick

- Ease of use – Ideal for beginners, non-stick woks don't require seasoning, making clean-up quick and simple.

- Lower heat requirement – Non-stick woks don't need extremely high temperatures to cook food effectively, which can be a plus for home cooks using standard stovetops.

- Shorter lifespan – Over time, non-stick coatings wear down or get damaged, especially when exposed to high heat or metal utensils, which limits the wok's longevity.

While both types of wok have their merits, it all comes down to your cooking style, experience level and how often you expect to use it. Start small and you can upgrade later as your cooking style evolves.

The chopping board

A good chopping board is vital in any kitchen: if your ingredients are the stars of the show, the chopping board is their stage. As well as protecting your worktops, the right chopping board will improve the longevity of your knives. Plastic boards are cheap, low-maintenance and will work fine in a pinch, but they tend to scratch easily and, over time, those grooves can harbour bacteria. When the time comes to replace your chopping board, here's what to consider:

Material:

- Wooden boards, especially hardwood boards like maple, walnut and cherry, are gentle on knives, ensuring they stay sharp for longer. They also have natural antibacterial properties. However, they do require regular oiling to prevent drying out or cracking.
- Eco-friendly and harder than most woods, bamboo boards resist deep scratches and are relatively easy to maintain.
- Made of a combination of wood fibres and resin, composite boards offer a middle ground between wood and plastic. They're tough, knife-friendly and often dishwasher-safe.

Size: Opt for a size that suits both the workspace in your kitchen and your style of cooking. If space allows, having a large board can make tasks like chopping veggies or breaking down protein sources more efficient.

Maintenance: Some boards require regular oiling or special cleaning methods to keep them in top shape.

The best chopping board for your kitchen ultimately depends on your preferences, and what else you have in your kitchen – if you only have beginner's knives, for example, you don't need to spend a fortune on a wooden board to keep them sharp. Whatever you choose, ensure it provides a stable surface and that you care for it appropriately.

The chef's knife for East Asian cooking – the chopper

When it comes to culinary knives, the chef's knife often reigns supreme. But when it comes to East Asian cooking, the 'chopper' (also known as the Chinese cleaver or Chinese chef's knife) holds special significance.

Unlike slender, Western chef's knives, the chopper has a rectangular blade, resembling a cleaver but with a thinner profile. This design makes it incredibly versatile: its wide blade is suitable for slicing, dicing and mincing. The side of the blade is perfect for crushing ingredients like garlic, while the flat surface can transport cut ingredients from board to wok.

Despite its broad appearance, the chopper can also be precise. Its design facilitates thin slicing – crucial for many East Asian dishes.

Typically made from carbon steel or stainless steel, choppers are robust and can withstand years of use, so if you're looking to upgrade your knives, a good chopper is a worthy investment.

Choosing and maintaining a chopper

- Choose the right material for your needs. Carbon steel holds a sharp edge longer but requires more care to prevent rusting. Stainless steel is more resistant to rust but might need sharpening more frequently.
- Ensure the handle is comfortable for your grip. Traditionally handles were made of wood, but modern versions often use plastic.
- The blade and handle should feel balanced when you hold the knife, meaning you can cut efficiently and without getting tired.
- Like all knives, choppers should be sharpened regularly to maintain their edge. Hand-washing and drying immediately (especially for carbon steel) will prolong their lifespan and prevent rusting.

A quality chopper is an investment, and with proper maintenance it could just last you years.

WOK COOKING TECHNIQUES

The wok is an iconic part of East Asian cookery. By mastering these classic techniques, you'll be well on your way to recreating authentic Chinese dishes at home.

Stir-frying (炒, chǎo)
This is the quintessential wok cooking method, where ingredients are cooked quickly over a high heat while being constantly stirred.

To stir-fry, heat the wok until it's smoking hot. Add a small amount of oil, followed by aromatics (e.g. garlic and ginger), then proteins and, finally, vegetables. By adding ingredients based on their cooking times, everything is ready simultaneously, and each ingredient maintains the perfect texture.

Note: Speed is essential. The wok must remain hot, and ingredients must be stirred continuously to ensure even cooking without burning.

Shallow-frying (煎, jiān)
Ingredients are fried in a small amount of oil, enough to cover the bottom half of the food.

To shallow-fry, heat the wok and add more oil than for stir-frying but less than for deep-frying. Once the oil is hot, add the ingredients. This method is often used for items like dumplings or fish to ensure they become golden and crispy.

Note: Flip the ingredients occasionally to ensure even browning. Control the heat to prevent burning.

Deep-frying (炸, zhá)
Food is submerged entirely in hot oil to achieve a crispy exterior and fully cooked interior.

To deep-fry, half-fill the wok with oil and heat until a deep-fry thermometer reads the temperature stated in the recipe (usually between 175–190°C/345–375°F). Add the food, ensuring you don't overcrowd the wok. You may need to work in batches.

Note: Use a slotted spoon or wire strainer to remove food once golden and crispy. Always be careful to avoid splashes and splatters when using hot oil.

Braising (炖, dùn)
This method involves an initial searing or frying stage, followed by slow cooking in liquid. Ideal for tougher cuts of meat, braising tenderizes tough proteins and allows the flavours to develop.

First sear the meat or vegetables in a hot wok to lock in flavour – you want caramelization – then add the liquid (like broth, sauce or water). Simmer over a low heat until the ingredients are tender and the flavours melded.

Note: You will need to check the liquid levels regularly and top up as needed.

By mastering these techniques, you're well on your way to authentically recreating the depth and variety found in traditionally prepared Chinese food.

EASY KITCHEN HACKS

When it comes to Chinese cooking, swift movements and impeccable timing are paramount. While the kitchen is a space brimming with flavours and aromas, it can also be home to the stresses of time constraints. The kitchen hacks in this section will streamline your culinary adventures, making the journey from prep to plating a breeze, and ensuring your time in the kitchen is more joy than chore.

1. BULK MINCE YOUR AROMATICS

Devote some time to mincing garlic, ginger and chilli in bulk. Once minced, portion the aromatics into practical, recipe-sized quantities and freeze them. There's no need to defrost them before use.

This not only saves you prep time later, but also ensures you always have these essential ingredients to hand, ready to catapult your dishes to new aromatic heights.

2. COOK ONCE, EAT TWICE

Don't let leftover rice go to waste. Portion it up and then freeze it – but for safety reasons, only freeze rice that's been cooled quickly (if it's been left out for hours or overnight, throw it out) and make sure you never reheat rice more than once.

By doing this, you're not just saving money by minimizing waste; you're also guaranteeing a convenient, quick fix for future meals. Reheated rice can seamlessly slide into fried rice recipes or be an accompaniment to saucy dishes.

3. PART-FREEZE FOR PRECISION

If you need to thinly slice meat, partially freeze it to make the slicing process smoother.

This tip is golden: the partial freeze provides structure, allowing for cleaner, thinner slices, which ensure even, uniform cooking.

4. MASTER THE ART OF VELVETING

This technique involves marinating the meat in a mixture of cornflour (cornstarch), egg white and rice vinegar, then blanching it in water or oil. It's an essential part of Chinese cooking that creates that melt-in-your-mouth tenderness.

Follow the velveting instructions on page 95 or 99, then portion out the velveted meat and freeze it.

The advantage? Having velveted meat on hand not only fast-tracks your cooking process but also guarantees dishes with tender, succulent meat every time.

Each of these hacks is a stepping stone towards cooking more efficiently, which, in turn, means you can have more fun in the kitchen. By integrating them into your kitchen routine, you embrace not just the flavours and techniques of East Asian cooking but also its inherent wisdom – the understanding that good cooking is not just about the end product but also about the harmony, balance and efficiency of the process. Happy wok-ing!

EASY KITCHEN GADGETS

While not traditional features of a home Chinese kitchen, there are a multitude of appliances that can take your cooking to new heights.

THE PRESSURE COOKER

Pressure cookers are worth having in the kitchen: they speed up cooking by using high pressure to raise the internal temperature. You can find stovetop and electric versions, but both essentially work in the same way. They seal steam inside a lockable lid, cooking food quickly while preserving flavours, colours and nutrients.

Pressure cookers are excellent for quickly tenderizing tough meats, and they're also great for stews, soups, beans and dense vegetables. They're especially effective for soups and broths.

You will find a pressure cooker recipe on page 69, but you can adapt any of the braises and stews to this cooking method, if you like. You may need to experiment with the timings at first, but use the manufacturer's manual as a guide.

THE AIR FRYER

Air fryers are incredibly popular at the moment, and for good reason. Air fryers work by circulating hot air around the food at high speed, cooking the food and producing a crispy layer, similar to deep-frying but with significantly less fat, all while being more efficient.

If you already have an air fryer, you'll find a selection of recipes on pages 48, 86, 104, 121 and 125. If you don't, consider getting a multicooker that allows you to pressure cook, too, for all the benefits outlined above.

THE RICE COOKER

A rice cooker is a godsend for households who regularly eat rice! It is essentially a dedicated kitchen appliance designed to cook rice perfectly every time – which takes out all of the usual pot watching and clean up. It works by using a combination of heat, a cooking bowl and a timer to control the cooking process automatically. It also switches to a 'keep warm' mode once the rice is cooked, so it doesn't overcook or stick.

It's easy to find rice cookers in a variety of sizes and price points. It will come down to how you plan to use it. A good non-stick inner pot can be easier to clean, for example, if you're using it regularly, and you might want additional features for cooking different types of rice (white, brown, sushi) or even cooking porridge, steaming vegetables or heating soup. Again, it's possible to buy multicookers with a rice-cooker function, which can make life easier.

All appliances vary, so follow the manufacturer's instructions to ensure you get perfect rice every time.

starters and small plates

CRISPY CHEESY CRAB WONTONS

Serves 4

Preparation time: 15 minutes

Cooking time: 4 minutes

24 wonton skins

Vegetable oil

Dipping sauce of your choice

For the filling

300g (10½oz) crab sticks, finely chopped

75g (2½oz) onion, finely diced

75g (2½oz) carrot, peeled and finely diced

75g (2½oz) spring onions (scallions), finely diced

Pinch of salt

180–200g (6–7oz) cream cheese

Looking for an irresistible combination of crispy shells and creamy, cheesy crab filling? Then look no further for a symphony of flavour in every bite!

Place all the filling ingredients in a large bowl and mix very well.

Separate the wonton skins, then take one skin and place roughly half a tablespoon of filling in the middle. Pinch in the four sides so they meet in the middle, creating a star-like shape. Repeat with the remaining wonton skins and filling.

In a wok or deep saucepan, heat 7.5–10cm (3–4in) of oil to around 180°C (350°F), then add the wontons in batches and fry until golden brown and cooked all the way through. This will take around 4 minutes per batch. Remove the cooked wontons and allow to drain and cool slightly before serving.

Serve with your favourite dipping sauce and enjoy.

GOLDEN CHICKEN AND SWEETCORN DUMPLINGS

Serves 4

Preparation time: 15 minutes

Cooking time: 10 minutes

20 round dumpling wrappers

2 tbsp vegetable oil

For the filling

450g (1lb) minced (ground) chicken

3 spring onions (scallions), finely chopped

90g (½ cup) sweetcorn

1 tbsp minced garlic

½ tbsp minced ginger

½ tbsp sesame oil

2 tbsp cornflour (cornstarch)

½ tsp salt

Pinch of white pepper

2 tsp chicken powder

For the sauce

2 tsp cornflour (cornstarch)

1 tbsp oyster sauce

2 tsp light soy sauce

3 tbsp water

1 tsp sesame oil

½ tbsp vegetable oil

These plump little dumplings are filled with tender chicken, sweetcorn and aromatic seasonings, then pan-fried to gain their sticky bottoms and served with a fragrant sesame-infused sauce. Perfect as a starter or a movie night snack.

Combine all the filling ingredients, then using a teaspoon, place a spoonful of filling in the centre of each dumpling wrapper. Dab a little bit of water on the top edge of the wrapper and then bring top and bottom together and pinch to seal while squeezing out any excess air. Repeat until all the filling has been used.

In a bowl, combine all the sauce ingredients and then set to one side.

Heat a frying pan (skillet) or wok over a medium heat, add the oil and place your dumplings into the oil (bottom-side down). Fry the dumplings until the bottoms have turned a golden brown, then add half a cup of water to the pan and cover with a lid and cook for 5 minutes until the water has evaporated, steaming the dumplings. Finally add the sauce mixture to the pan and cook until the sauce has evaporated, leaving the dumplings with sticky bottoms. Transfer to a serving plate and enjoy with your favourite dipping sauce.

PAN-FRIED NORI DUMPLINGS

Serves 4

Preparation time: 15 minutes

Cooking time: 10 minutes

20–22 sheets of nori, cut into 8 x 6cm (3¼ x 2½in) pieces

2 tbsp vegetable oil

For the filling

450g (1lb) minced (ground) chicken

Bunch of spring onions (scallions), finely chopped

2 tbsp minced garlic

1 tbsp minced ginger

½ tbsp sesame oil

2 tbsp cornflour (cornstarch)

½ tsp salt

Pinch of ground black pepper

2 tsp chicken powder

Indulge in these delectable gluten-free nori dumplings! Packed with minced (ground) chicken, spring onions (scallions) and a huge burst of flavour, they're quick to prepare and perfect for dipping.

Thoroughly mix all the filling ingredients together, then place in a disposable piping bag. Pipe the mixture along one of the short sides of a piece of nori and roll to make a cylinder. Repeat until all the filling has been used.

Heat a frying pan (skillet) or wok over a medium heat and fry the rolls in the oil for 6–8 minutes until the filling is cooked all the way through.

Transfer to a serving plate and eat with your favourite dipping sauce.

SUPER CRISPY KING PRAWN DIM SUM

Serves 4

Preparation time: 15 minutes

Cooking time: 5 minutes

12 wonton skins

Vegetable oil, for frying

Dipping sauce of your choice (I recommend salad cream)

For the filling

450g (1lb) raw king prawns (jumbo shrimp), peeled and deveined

2 garlic cloves, crushed

½ tsp salt

¼ tsp white pepper

1½ tbsp oyster sauce

2 tbsp cornflour (cornstarch)

These super crispy dumplings deliver the perfect combination of crunchy succulence. In just 20 minutes, you can whip up these delectable bites, bursting with prawn (shrimp) goodness. Perfectly crunchy on the outside, tender on the inside and served with your choice of dipping sauce. Delightful!

Place all the filling ingredients into a blender and, using the pulse function, blend until you have a smooth paste. Transfer to a bowl, cover with cling film (plastic wrap) and place in the fridge for 1 hour. This process is not vital if you're short on time, but it does help make the next step easier.

Separate the wonton skins, then slice them into thin strips. Once cut, mix them all together on a clean plate so that they resemble noodles.

Remove the prawn mixture from the fridge and then, using a tablespoon, form bite-sized balls of mixture. Place a ball of filling on to the plate of cut wonton skins. Now carefully coat the ball in wonton skins and set to one side. Repeat until all the prawn mixture has been used.

In a deep-sided saucepan, heat 7.5–10cm (3–4in) of oil to about 180°C (350°F) and fry the dim sum balls in batches of about 5 or 6 until golden brown and cooked all the way through. This will take 4–5 minutes for each batch. Remove the cooked dim sum balls and allow to drain and cool slightly before serving.

Serve with your favourite dipping sauce and enjoy.

FRIED YAKI ONIGIRI

Serves 2

Preparation time: 5 minutes

Cooking time: 35 minutes

2 tbsp vegetable oil

5 sheets of nori, chopped into about 12 x 5cm (4½ x 2in) pieces

For the rice
300g (1⅓ cups) sushi rice

1 tbsp rice vinegar

2 tbsp mirin

Pinch of salt

2 tbsp toasted sesame seeds

For the glaze
2 tbsp light soy sauce

1 tbsp dark soy sauce

1 tbsp mirin

2 tsp sugar

In China, it's popular to combine rice with various seasonings and fillings to make Chinese fried rice cakes or rice balls. This concept has evolved in different ways in different East Asian countries, and here I present my take on the irresistible delight of fried yaki onigiri – Japanese-style golden rice triangles, glazed with a rich soy sauce blend, encased in nori for a crispy, savoury and satisfying treat. A culinary journey awaits you!

Wash the rice under warm water until the water runs clear – this normally takes 3–4 rinses. Place the rice into a rice cooker or saucepan. Add enough water so it sits about 2cm (¾in) above the top of the rice. Turn your rice cooker on and put on the lid. If you are boiling your rice, cook in a saucepan over a medium-high heat until all the water has been absorbed. Switch off the heat and cover with a tight lid. Now leave it alone for 15 minutes.

Once your rice is cooked and rested, add the rice vinegar, mirin, salt and sesame seeds and mix well.

In a separate bowl, mix all the glaze ingredients together.

Form the rice into 6cm (2½in) triangles, roughly 3–4cm (1¼–1½in) thick. Once all the rice has been shaped, heat a wok over a medium-high heat and add the oil. Place the rice triangles into the hot oil and after 1 minute of cooking on each side, begin to brush the rice with the glaze. Continue to fry on all sides until golden brown and crispy, ensuring you brush frequently to build up a delicious soy glaze.

Place a piece of nori flat on a chopping board, then sit a piece of cooked onigiri in the centre of the nori and wrap the sides up towards the triangle point. Repeat with all the rice pieces.

CRISPY CHICKEN SPRING ROLLS

Serves 6–8

Preparation time: 30 minutes

Cooking time: 5 minutes

Bunch of spring onions (scallions), roughly chopped

1 large carrot, peeled and roughly chopped

4 garlic cloves, roughly chopped

600g (1lb 5oz) minced (ground) chicken

2 tbsp light soy sauce

2 tbsp fish sauce

2 tsp chicken powder

Pinch of white pepper

1 packet of Chinese spring roll wrappers (the mixture makes about 20–30 rolls, depending on how generous you are with the filling)

1 egg, beaten, for egg wash

Vegetable oil, for frying

Chilli sauce, to serve

These satisfyingly crunchy, crispy delights are filled with a savoury minced (ground) chicken mixture, perfect for dipping in your favourite chilli sauce.

Begin by adding the spring onions, carrot and garlic to a food processor, then blend until you have a finely chopped mixture.

Add the minced chicken and the blended veg to a bowl and then add the soy sauce, fish sauce, chicken powder and white pepper. Mix until you have a slightly sticky paste and everything is completely combined.

For ease, you can now transfer the mixture into a piping bag and set to one side.

Separate the spring roll wrappers, then take one sheet and pipe an 8cm (3¼in) long sausage roughly a quarter of the way up the wrapper. Fold the end nearest to you over the sausage creating a cylinder, then fold the sides in to seal in the mixture. Continue to roll until you have a cylinder, then egg wash the last 3cm (1¼in) and continue to roll until you have a spring roll. Repeat until all the filling mixture has been used up.

If wanted, now you can freeze your spring rolls ready for when you need them and, yes, they can be fried from frozen.

When ready to cook, take a deep-sided pan and heat some oil to 180°C (350°F). You want enough oil to submerge the spring rolls without them sitting on the bottom of the pan. Fry the spring rolls in batches until golden brown and cooked all the way through. This takes about 5–6 minutes. Drain and allow to cool for 5 minutes before eating. Serve with your favourite chilli sauce.

PHOENIX ROLLS

Serves 4

Preparation time: 25 minutes

Cooking time: 10 minutes

150g (5½oz) raw king prawns (jumbo shrimp), peeled and deveined

3 eggs

2 tsp cornflour (cornstarch)

3 tbsp milk

1 tbsp butter

6 slices of fresh white bread

¼ x 340g (11¾oz) can of Spam, cut into 6 strips

Vegetable oil, for frying

Introducing the irresistible phoenix rolls! While their origin may be a culinary mystery, I'm confident that this recipe will become a family favourite. Picture this: crispy fried bread enveloping king prawns (jumbo shrimp), succulent Spam slices and tender egg, all complemented by your favourite dipping sauce. Trust me, you don't want to miss out on this mouthwatering delight.

Mince the king prawns, either chopping into a paste by hand or quickly blitzing in a blender.

Break the eggs into a bowl, add the cornflour and milk and whisk together.

Heat a frying pan (skillet) or wok over a medium heat, add the butter and then gently cook the eggs until you have an omelette. Remove from the pan, and once cooled, chop it into 6 slices.

Remove the crusts from the bread and, using a rolling pin, flatten the bread slices by a third. Set to one side.

Lay the bread on a flat surface, then cover each slice in the prawn mixture. Lay a strip of spam a third of the way up the slice of bread, followed by a slice of omelette. Starting from the edge closest to you, roll the bread over the ingredients to form a cylinder.

Heat a medium saucepan (large enough to place the rolls into) over a medium-high heat and add enough oil to shallow-fry the rolls. Once the oil temperature has reached around 180°C (350°F), carefully place the rolls into the oil and cook for 2–3 minutes, or until golden brown all over. You'll need to flip them a couple of times during cooking to ensure even browning. Transfer on to paper towels and allow to cool for 5 minutes. Cut each roll into 5 equal pieces and serve with your favourite dipping sauce.

SALT AND PEPPER AUBERGINE FRITTERS

Serves 2–4

Preparation time: 10 minutes

Cooking time: 15 minutes

For the fritters

2 aubergines (eggplants)

1 tsp salt

3 eggs

1 tbsp English mustard

3 tbsp Japanese kewpie mayonnaise (or normal mayo)

60g (1 cup) panko breadcrumbs

125g (1 cup) plain (all-purpose) flour

Pinch of white pepper

1 tsp chilli powder of your choice

120ml (½ cup) vegetable oil

For the topping

1 tsp salt

1 tsp ground black pepper

1 tsp Chinese five spice

With crispy, golden exteriors and tender insides, these fritters are the perfect blend of flavour and texture, topped with a tantalizing seasoning. Serve these irresistible fritters as a snack or a teaser at the start of a meal.

Peel the aubergines, keeping the stems attached, then slice into 1.5cm (⅝in) thick slices. Cut each slice into 1cm (¾in) fingers, ensuring you don't go quite as high as the stem, as you want the slices of aubergine to resemble a hand with fingers.

Place the aubergine slices into a saucepan of water along with the salt, cover with a lid and poach for 5 minutes or until just tender. Remove from the water and allow to drain.

Combine the eggs, mustard and mayonnaise, mixing well.

In a separate bowl, combine the panko breadcrumbs, flour, white pepper and chilli powder.

In a wok or deep-sided frying pan (skillet), heat the oil over a medium heat and, once the oil has reached 170–180°C (340–350°F), maintain the temperature.

Dredge each piece of poached aubergine in the flour mixture, then dip into the egg mixture. Shallow-fry the aubergine in the oil until golden brown and super tender, yet crispy on the outside. Drain and set to one side.

Combine all the topping ingredients and sprinkle over the cooked fritters.

RAMEN RICE DUMPLINGS

Serves 2

Preparation time: 5 minutes

Cooking time: 15 minutes

2 packets of instant ramen noodles (use your favourite)

4 sheets of dried rice paper

4 slices of American sliced cheese

1 sheet of nori, cut into quarters

2 tbsp vegetable oil

Ramen is a classic example of Japanese Chinese cuisine. It's believed to have travelled from 1800s China to Chinatown in Yokohama, Japan, and it's now eaten in every region of Japan. In that spirit, this is a modern fusion dish. Tender ramen noodles, gooey American cheese and nori wrapped in delicate rice paper, then fried until golden. A delicately wrapped gift for your taste buds!

Cook the ramen noodles following the instructions on the packet. If you are using soupy noodles, use less water as you want the noodles less soupy for this recipe.

Place a piece of rice paper in water for 5 seconds, then on to a chopping board. Take a slice of American cheese and lay it in the centre of the rice paper. Top the cheese with some noodles, then place a slice of nori on top of the noodles. Fold the sides of the rice paper over the filling, creating a sealed parcel or dumpling. Repeat until all the noodles have been used.

Place a wok or frying pan (skillet) over a medium-high heat and add the oil, then fry the dumplings until golden brown on both sides, ensuring they don't touch each other as they fry, or they will stick together. Serve with your favourite dipping sauce.

TOFU NORI BITES WITH SWEET CHILLI SAUCE

Serves 2

Preparation time: 10 minutes

Cooking time: 12 minutes

300g (10½oz) firm tofu, cut into 4 x 2cm (1½ x ¾in) pieces

2 sheets of nori, cut into 2cm (¾in) thick strips

60g (½ cup) cornflour (cornstarch)

2 tbsp vegetable oil

2 tbsp toasted sesame seeds

For the sauce

½ tbsp light soy sauce

1 tsp dark soy sauce

½ tbsp Chinese rice wine (Shaoxing wine)

4 tbsp sweet chilli sauce

2 tbsp water

Experience the delightful fusion of textures and flavours of these nori-wrapped tofu bites. Crispy on the outside, silky tofu on the inside, all dressed in a tantalizing sweet chilli sauce. A quick, easy and incredibly tasty snack.

Combine all the sauce ingredients in a bowl, mixing well.

Wrap each piece of tofu in a strip of nori, then dredge in the cornflour, shaking off any excess.

Heat the oil in a wok or frying pan (skillet) over a medium heat and fry the tofu, turning frequently until golden brown. Now add the sauce and gently bring to the boil, ensuring you turn the pieces of tofu in the sauce so they are well coated. Finally, sprinkle over the sesame seeds and serve.

STEAMED BITE-SIZED SPARE RIBS

Serves 2

Preparation time: 30 minutes

Cooking time: 20 minutes

450g (1lb) pork ribs, cut into bite-sized pieces

1 tbsp rice vinegar

1 tsp salt

1 tsp sesame oil

3 spring onions (scallions), finely chopped

For the marinade

2 tbsp light soy sauce

1 tbsp minced ginger

1 tbsp minced garlic

Pinch of salt

Pinch of white pepper

2 tsp cornflour (cornstarch)

2 tbsp black bean sauce

2 tbsp vegetable oil

Succulent pork ribs expertly marinated in a mixture of ginger, garlic and black bean sauce, then steamed to tender perfection. A dish that's sure to satisfy your taste buds.

Place the ribs in a large bowl along with the vinegar and salt, then cover with water and massage for 1 minute. Soak the ribs for a further 20 minutes. This process will help remove any impurities from the ribs and also tenderize the meat.

Drain the ribs and allow to dry thoroughly, then place into a heatproof bowl along with all the marinade ingredients, except the oil. Massage the ribs for 1–2 minutes, ensuring that the ribs are well coated in the marinade and thoroughly mixed. Now add the oil, which will help lock in moisture as the ribs cook.

Place the ribs into a steamer and steam over a medium-high heat for 20 minutes. Once cooked, remove the ribs from the steamer, arrange on a serving plate and top with the sesame oil and chopped spring onions.

Delicious as a meaty snack or as part of a main meal.

CHEESY KIMCHI RICE BALLS

Serves 2

Preparation time: 7 minutes

Cooking time: 6 minutes

250–300g (9–10½oz) packet of pre-cooked sticky rice (or you can cook your own)

65g (½ cup) kimchi, finely chopped

2 tbsp gochujang

1 tsp sesame oil

175g (¾ cup) grated mozzarella

2 tbsp vegetable oil

1 sheet of nori, cut into 3 strips, then each strip cut in half

In Korean and Chinese food culture alike, fermented, spicy foods are popular, so I love experimenting with Korean ingredients. Kimchi well-loved across the globe, and while pairing it with rice and cheesy goodness is non-traditional, it's a modern flavour combination that works! Bursting with umami from the kimchi and oozing with molten mozzarella, these irresistible rice balls are a quick and easy treat that will leave you craving more.

Open the packet of cooked sticky rice and empty it into a bowl, then add the chopped kimchi, gochujang and sesame oil and mix well. Lightly dampen your hands and divide the mixture into 6 equal parts. Roll each piece into a ball and then, using your finger, press a well into each ball. Fill the well with cheese and then mould the rice around the cheese, sealing it inside. Shape into a fat triangle. Repeat until all the balls are filled and shaped.

Brush each triangle with a little oil, then place in an air fryer and cook at 180°C (350°F) for 6 minutes, or until heated all the way through and the cheese has melted. Alternatively, you can gently pan-fry the triangles until heated all the way through. Once cooked, wrap each triangle with a piece of nori and serve.

CHILLI AND SALT CHIPS

Serves 4

Preparation time: 5 minutes

Cooking time: 5 minutes, plus time to cook your chips

750g (1lb 10oz) oven chips (thick or thin, crinkled or straight, it really is your choice)

For the topping

1 tsp salt

1 tsp ground black pepper

1 tsp dried chilli flakes

1 tsp Chinese five spice

1 tbsp vegetable oil

1 onion, finely diced

1 green (bell) pepper, finely diced (or use your favourite colour)

1 tbsp roughly chopped garlic

2 or 3 bird's eye chillies, finely chopped

These chilli and salt chips, a beloved British–Chinese takeaway staple, tantalize the taste buds with their irresistible combination of crispy fries, fiery chilli heat and savoury saltiness. Discover the UK's spicy obsession in every bite.

Cook your chips; simply follow the instructions on the packet or make your own.

In a bowl, combine the salt, black pepper, chilli flakes and Chinese five spice and mix well.

Place a wok over a medium-high heat, then add the oil, along with the diced onion and (bell) pepper and cook until tender. Add the garlic and fry until fragrant. This is the time to open your windows and turn up the extractor fan... Add the chopped chillies, toss quickly and then add the cooked chips. Keep tossing and, as you toss, start sprinkling in your dry spice mixture. Once you've added all the spice, enjoy!

Chef's Tip

You can, of course, make your own chips in a deep-fat fryer or an air fryer and use those.

braises and stews

BRAISED CHICKEN WITH GINGER AND SPRING ONIONS

Serves 2

Preparation time: 10 minutes

Cooking time: 40 minutes

2 tbsp vegetable oil
2 tbsp sugar
1½ tbsp minced garlic
3–4 slices of ginger
8 spring onions (scallions), cut into 5cm- (2in-) long strips
1 small onion, finely diced
450g (1lb) skin-on, boneless chicken thighs, cut into bite-sized strips
2 tbsp oyster sauce
1 tbsp light soy sauce
½ tbsp dark soy sauce
¼ tsp white pepper
Salt, to taste

Tender chicken strips marinated to perfection, served in a savoury sauce with a hint of sweetness. A deliciously simple dish!

Place a wok over a medium heat, add the oil and sugar but do not stir. Once the sugar has begun to brown and darken, add the garlic, ginger, spring onions and onion and cook for a few seconds until fragrant. Now add the chicken and give everything a really good mix, then pour in 350ml (1½ cups) of water and the remaining ingredients, except the salt. Ensure all the ingredients are well combined and then reduce the heat to a simmer, cover and cook for 25 minutes.

Remove the lid and if the sauce is still quite thin, continue to cook until it begins to thicken. Check the seasoning and add salt if required. Finally, transfer to a serving plate and enjoy with your favourite vegetable sides.

GLASS NOODLE CHICKEN STEW

Serves 4

Preparation time: 5 minutes, plus 1 hour marinating

Cooking time: 20 minutes

300g (10½oz) boneless, skinless chicken thighs, cut into bite sized pieces

For the marinade

1 tbsp doubanjiang

2 tbsp oyster sauce

1 tbsp kecap manis (sweet soy sauce)

1 tbsp Chinese rice wine (Shaoxing wine) or dry sherry

1 tbsp sugar

For the stew

120g (4¼oz) dried glass noodles (mung bean noodles)

1 tbsp vegetable oil

3 garlic cloves, crushed and bruised

3–4 slices of ginger

Bunch of spring onions (scallions), cut into 5cm (2in) lengths

12 dried red chillies

1½ tbsp chicken powder

150g (5½oz) Chinese leaf (Napa cabbage), cut into chunks

150g (5½oz) pak choi (bok choy), cut into chunks

80g (2¾oz) shiitake mushrooms, cut into bite-sized pieces

Salt and white pepper, to taste

Delve into the bold symphony of flavours of this chicken stew! Marinated chicken, vibrant vegetables and delicate glass noodles harmonize in a rich and satisfying culinary crescendo.

Begin by placing the chicken and all the marinade ingredients in a bowl, then massage them thoroughly into the meat and set to one side to marinate for 1 hour.

Soak the glass noodles in cold water and set to one side.

In a deep wok or large saucepan over a medium-high heat, add the oil, then add the garlic, ginger, spring onions and chillies and fry until fragrant. Now add the marinated chicken and fry for a further 3–4 minutes. Next, add the chicken powder along with 750ml (3¼ cups) of water and mix well. As the stew is coming to the boil, arrange the Chinese leaf, pak choi and mushrooms on the top of the stew, cover with the lid and, once boiling, reduce the heat to a simmer. After 5 minutes, drain the glass noodles and add to the pan. Gently push the noodles into the stew and then place the lid back on and simmer for a further 8 minutes. Finally, give everything a gentle stir, check the seasoning and adjust to taste with salt and white pepper.

Serve the entire pot in the middle of the table.

AROMATIC BRAISED BEEF STEW

Serves: 4

Preparation time: 10 minutes

Cooking time: 2 hours 30 minutes

- 2 tbsp vegetable oil
- 600g (1lb 5oz) beef brisket, cut into 2.5cm (1in) cubes
- 2 onions, thinly sliced
- 3 spring onions (scallions), roughly chopped
- 2 carrots, peeled and roughly chopped
- 7 cloves
- 3 star anise
- Small piece of cinnamon stick
- 2 bay leaves
- 1 tbsp chicken powder
- 120ml (½ cup) Chinese rice wine (Shaoxing wine) or dry sherry
- 120ml (½ cup) mirin
- 3 tbsp light soy sauce
- 2 tbsp oyster sauce
- 1 tsp cornflour (cornstarch), mixed with 2 tsp water (optional)

Indulge in the enticing symphony of flavours of my aromatic braised beef stew: tender cubes of beef cocooned in a rich medley of fragrant spices, onions and carrots. Slowly simmered to perfection, this hearty dish promises an exquisite fusion of textures and tastes that will warm your soul.

Place a saucepan over a medium heat, then add the oil and cook the beef cubes until browned. Remove and set to one side.

Add the onions and spring onions to the pan and fry for 2–3 minutes until translucent and slightly caramelized. Now add the carrots, cloves, star anise, cinnamon stick, bay leaves and chicken powder and give everything a good mix.

Next, add the wet ingredients: rice wine, mirin, soy sauce, oyster sauce and 1 litre (4 cups) of water, then, once bubbling, add the beef, reduce the heat to low, cover and cook for 1½–2 hours.

Remove the lid and cook over a low heat for a further 30 minutes until the sauce has reduced by a third. If you'd like to thicken your sauce, add the cornflour mixture and stir this into your sauce.

This unctuous beef dish is best served on top of rice or noodles, or it makes the best filled baguette you've ever eaten.

BRAISED SPARE RIBS

Serves 2–4

Preparation time: 5 minutes

Cooking time: 65 minutes

450–600g (1lb–1lb 5oz) pork ribs, separated into individual ribs

For the sauce

3 slices of ginger

3 spring onions (scallions)

3 star anise

1 cinnamon stick

6 dried chillies

500–600ml (generous 2½ cups) rice beer

1 tbsp light soy sauce

½ tbsp dark soy sauce

2 tbsp oyster sauce

5 tbsp tomato ketchup

3 tbsp brown sauce

2 tbsp sugar

Deliciously tender braised spare ribs simmered to melting point in a fragrant blend of ginger, spring onions (scallions), star anise, cinnamon and dried chillies. They are served in a rich sauce, which creates a mouthwateringly sticky glaze.

Place the ribs in a large saucepan, cover with cold water, then place over a medium-high heat and bring to the boil. As the water begins to boil, start to skim off any impurities that float to the top. Continue to cook for 25 minutes.

Drain the ribs and set to one side to cool.

Once the ribs have cooled, place all the sauce ingredients in a wok or saucepan, mix well and then add the blanched ribs. Place the pan over a medium heat and gently bring to a light boil, then reduce the heat, pop on the lid and cook for a further 35 minutes. Remove the lid and allow the sauce to reduce by a third.

Transfer to a serving plate and enjoy.

CARAMELIZED BRAISED PORK BELLY

Serves 4

Preparation time: 10 minutes

Cooking time: 1 hour

2 tbsp vegetable oil

500g (1lb 2oz) pork belly, skin removed and cut into 3cm (1¼in) cubes

2 tbsp sugar

1½ tbsp minced garlic

5 spring onions (scallions), finely chopped (greens and whites separated)

1 small onion, finely diced

2 tbsp fish sauce

2 tbsp oyster sauce

½ tbsp dark soy sauce

1 tsp onion powder

¼ tsp white pepper

A tantalizing dish featuring succulent cubes of pork belly infused with rich sweet and savoury flavours. Tender, juicy and utterly delicious!

Place a wok over a medium-high heat, add 1 tablespoon of the oil, followed by the pork belly and brown on all sides. Once the pork belly is browned, pour over boiling water until covered and bring to the boil. Once boiling, reduce the heat to a simmer and cook for 30 minutes. Remove the wok from the heat and drain the pork.

Place a clean wok over a medium heat, then add the remaining oil along with the sugar but do not stir. Once the sugar has begun to brown and darken, add the garlic, spring onion whites and onion, cook for a few seconds and then add 350ml (1½ cups) of water and the remaining ingredients, except the spring onion greens. Add the pork belly, ensure all the ingredients are well combined, then reduce the heat to a simmer, cover and cook for a further 20 minutes.

Remove the lid and, if the sauce is still quite thin, continue to cook until it begins to thicken. Finally, transfer to a serving plate and top with the spring onion greens to serve.

SOY-BRAISED CHICKEN LEGS

Serves 2

Preparation time: 10 minutes, plus 20 minutes soaking and 20 minutes marinating

Cooking time: 25 minutes

pinch of salt

1 tbsp rice vinegar

2 skin-on chicken legs

3 slices of ginger

5 spring onions (scallions), cut into 5cm (2in) lengths (greens and whites separated)

3 tbsp light soy sauce

2 tbsp dark soy sauce

3 tbsp oyster sauce

1½ tbsp sugar

Unlock the culinary magic of braising with soy sauce. This time-honoured technique transforms any meat into a delectably tender delight.

Begin by placing the chicken in a large bowl along with a pinch of salt, rice vinegar and enough water to cover. Fully submerge the chicken and allow it to sit for 20 minutes in the water. This process will not only tenderize the meat but also remove any impurities. After 20 minutes, drain, then rinse and drain again. Pat dry. Place the chicken back into a clean bowl and add the ginger, half the spring onion greens, light and dark soy sauces, oyster sauce and sugar. Combine well and allow to marinate for 20 minutes.

Place the remaining spring onions into the bottom of a rice cooker or a medium saucepan, then place the chicken legs on top of the spring onions along with the marinade. Cover with the lid, turn the rice cooker on and cook for 25 minutes. If you are using a saucepan, gently bring the marinade to a simmer, reduce the heat to low, cover with the lid and cook for 25–30 minutes or until chicken is cooked all the way through.

Delicious served over steamed rice and drizzled with the cooking liquor.

BRAISED BLACK PEPPER BEEF

Serves 2

Preparation time: 5 minutes, plus 20 minutes marinating

Cooking time: 1½–2 hours

- 450g–500g (1lb–1lb 2oz) beef brisket, cut into 2.5cm (1in) cubes
- 2 tbsp vegetable oil
- 1 large onion, sliced
- 3 garlic cloves, crushed
- 1 green (bell) pepper, sliced
- 1 tbsp cornflour (cornstarch), mixed with 2 tbsp water

For the marinade

- ½ tbsp fish sauce
- ½ tbsp ground black pepper, plus extra for dressing the dish
- 3 tbsp oyster sauce

For the sauce

- 350ml (1½ cups) beef stock
- 1 tbsp light soy sauce
- ½ tbsp dark soy sauce
- 2 tbsp Chinese rice wine (Shaoxing wine)
- 1 tbsp brown sugar

Exquisitely succulent beef brisket, marinated and simmered in a robust sauce, pairs harmoniously with vegetables in this truly delightful dish. Enjoy with steamed rice.

Begin by marinating the beef; add all the marinade ingredients to a bowl and spend 1 minute massaging them into the beef. This process will help break down some of the muscle fibres, making the beef even more tender. Leave to marinate for 20 minutes.

Place a heavy saucepan over a medium-high heat, add the oil and then the marinated beef. Once browned on all sides, remove the beef and set to one side.

In the same pan, add the onion and cook until browned, then add the garlic along with the green pepper and cook for a further 1 minute or until fragrant. Now add the sauce ingredients, deglaze the bottom of the pan and return the browned beef to the pan. Once the sauce begins to come up to the boil, reduce the heat to very low, cover and cook for 1½ hours, or until the beef is super tender. (If your sauce begins to evaporate during this time, add more beef stock.) To finish, give the cornflour mixture a stir and slowly pour it into the sauce, stirring at the same time. Once the sauce thickens, switch off the heat.

Serve on top of freshly steamed rice with a final sprinkle of freshly ground black pepper.

TOFU AND MINCED PORK STEW

Serves 4

Preparation time: 10 minutes

Cooking time: 16–18 minutes

1 tbsp vegetable oil

5 spring onions (scallions), finely chopped

1 small onion, diced

300g (10½oz) minced (ground) pork (use a fattier mince if possible)

3 tbsp doubanjiang

1 tbsp fish sauce

2 tbsp rice vinegar

Pinch of ground black pepper

1 tbsp sugar

1 tbsp chicken powder

250g (9oz) silken tofu, cut into 2cm (¾in) cubes

2 tsp sesame oil

A flavourful harmony of savoury and spicy. Dive into a bowl of this comforting stew, where tender minced (ground) pork and silky tofu soak up the rich, aromatic flavours of chilli bean paste and tangy rice vinegar.

In a wok over a medium heat, add the oil and fry the spring onions and onion until translucent. Then add the pork and continue to fry until browned. Add the doubanjiang, fish sauce, vinegar, black pepper, sugar and chicken powder and mix well. Now add 1 litre (4 cups) of water and gently bring to the boil. Once boiling, reduce the heat to a simmer and gently add the silken tofu, being careful not to break up the delicate cubes. Allow to cook for a further 2–3 minutes, then switch off the heat and add the sesame oil. Stir gently so as not to break up the tofu too much and serve.

Delicious served over thick rice noodles.

BEEF KARE KARE

Serves 2–4

Preparation time: 10 minutes

Cooking time: 2 hours

- 450g (1lb) beef chuck, cut into thumb-sized cubes
- Pinch of salt
- Pinch of white pepper
- 2 tbsp vegetable oil, plus a little extra for roasting the vegetables
- 2 onions, thinly sliced
- 6 garlic cloves, minced
- 2 tbsp sweet paprika
- 2 tbsp fish sauce
- 1 beef stock cube (or you could use 1–2 tbsp chicken powder)
- 2 aubergines (eggplants), cut into thumb-sized cubes
- 125g (4½oz) green beans, cut into 7cm (2¾in) pieces (you can use long beans)
- 3 pak choi (bok choy), cut into bite-sized pieces
- 4 tbsp smooth peanut butter

Thanks to their similar geography, the rich tapestry of flavours and ingredients that define East and Southeast Asian cuisine often overlap. Beef kare kare is a traditional Filipino dish of tender beef cubes, seasoned and cooked in a savoury blend of onions, garlic and sweet paprika. Slow-cooked to perfection, it is elevated with creamy peanut butter, roasted aubergine, green beans and pak choi. I love to explore Filipino dishes as it shows me new ways with familiar ingredients. This is a mouthwatering treat for 2–4 people, perfect for special occasions or a comforting meal.

Season the beef cubes with the salt and white pepper, then fry in the oil until golden. Once browned all over, remove the beef from the pan and set to one side. Now, over a medium heat, fry the onions for 2–3 minutes until translucent, then add the garlic and fry until fragrant. Add the paprika, mix well, then pour in 1 litre (4 cups) of water to deglaze the bottom of the pan. Add the fish sauce and stock cube. Return the beef to the pan, reduce the heat to low, cover and cook for 1½ hours.

While the beef is cooking, roast the veggies in the oven. Preheat the oven to 160°C/325°F/Gas 3. Place the aubergines on a baking tray along with a little oil, then roast for 15 minutes. Now add the green beans, toss and place back in the oven for 5 minutes. Finally, add the pak choi, toss again and cook for a further 5 minutes. Remove from the oven and allow to cool on the tray.

Remove the beef from the saucepan, add the peanut butter and then using a hand blender, carefully blitz for 20–30 seconds until the curry is smooth. Return the beef to the pan along with the cooked aubergines, green beans and pak choi. Bring the curry back up to the boil and simmer for 2 minutes. Adjust the seasoning to your preference and serve over steamed rice.

PRESSURE-COOKER SWEET SOY SAUCE CHICKEN

Serves 4

Preparation time: 10 minutes

Cooking time: 50 minutes

- 3 tbsp dark soy sauce
- 1 large chicken (use a bird that will fit inside your pressure cooker)
- 3 spring onions (scallions), greens and whites separated
- 5 slices of ginger
- 2 tbsp vegetable oil
- 1 onion, roughly chopped
- 2 star anise
- Small piece of cinnamon stick
- 1 bay leaf
- 240ml (1 cup) light soy sauce
- 120ml (½ cup) Chinese rice wine (Shaoxing wine)
- 3 tbsp honey
- 2 tbsp brown sugar

Indulge in the delectable depths of sweet soy chicken. In less than 1 hour, you'll have tender, moist chicken, infused with rich soy and aromatic spices. Perfect for a hearty meal!

Begin by massaging 2 tablespoons of the dark soy sauce into the chicken skin, ensuring that you cover the entire bird. Now place the spring onion greens and 2 slices of the ginger into the cavity. Set the chicken to one side while you continue with the rest of the recipe.

Heat the pressure cooker and add the oil, along with the remaining ginger slices, spring onion whites and chopped onion and fry until fragrant and lightly browned. Now add the star anise, cinnamon and bay leaf and fry for a further minute.

Now it's time to add the wet ingredients; start by adding the light soy sauce, remaining dark soy sauce, rice wine, half a litre (2 cups) of water, the honey and lastly the sugar. Give everything a really good mix and gently bring to the boil. Now add the marinated chicken (breast-side down). Gently push the chicken into the liquid and, if needed, add another half a litre (2 cups) of water.

Place the lid on the pressure cooker and let it cook over a medium-high heat until it begins to whistle. Once it begins to whistle, reduce the heat slightly and cook for a further 10 minutes. Then turn off the heat and allow the chicken to cool and absorb the flavours for a further 15–20 minutes.

After cooling, remove the chicken from the pressure cooker, chop into bite-sized pieces and serve over freshly steamed rice with a side of Chinese vegetables and soy sauce for drizzling.

Important
Never fill your pressure cooker above two-thirds full.

chicken and prawns

SIMPLE CHICKEN TERIYAKI

Serves 2

Preparation time: 5 minutes

Cooking time: 10 minutes

350g (12oz) skin-on, boneless chicken thighs

1 tbsp oyster sauce

½ cup cornflour (cornstarch)

4 tbsp vegetable oil

For the sauce

3 tbsp light soy sauce

1 tbsp minced garlic

1 tbsp mirin

2 tbsp sugar

2 tsp chicken powder

Pinch of white pepper

Teriyaki is famously used in Japanese cuisine, and it's become popular throughout East Asia, including in Chinese cuisine. In the realm of speedy, satisfying dinners, this dish reigns supreme. In just 15 minutes, you can have a plate brimming with succulent chicken in delicious, glossy sauce. This recipe is your secret weapon for those busy weeknights when you crave something scrumptious without the fuss.

Place the chicken thighs in a bowl, add the oyster sauce and massage it into the chicken. Now dredge the chicken in the cornflour and shake off the excess. Place a wok over a medium heat, add the oil and fry the chicken until golden brown and cooked all the way through, remembering to turn frequently for even cooking.

Meanwhile, in a bowl, mix all the sauce ingredients together.

Once the chicken is cooked, remove it from the wok and, if you have any excess oil, wipe the wok with some paper towels to remove it. Pour in the sauce and heat gently. Once hot, add the cooked chicken and cook for a further 1–2 minutes.

Cut the chicken into bite-sized slices and serve over freshly steamed sticky white rice with your favourite veggies.

BLACK BEAN STEAMED CHICKEN

Serves 2

Preparation time: 8 minutes

Cooking time: 15–20 minutes

- 2 tbsp dried fermented black beans (or you could use a black bean paste)
- 450g (1lb) skin-on, boneless chicken thighs, cut into 2.5cm (1in) chunks
- 1 tbsp oyster sauce
- 1 tbsp light soy sauce
- ½ tbsp dark soy sauce
- ½ tbsp sugar
- 1 tbsp rice wine
- Thumb-sized piece of ginger, peeled and cut into thin matchsticks
- 1 tbsp minced garlic
- 1½ tbsp vegetable oil

This quick and easy dish serves two and pairs wonderfully with rice or noodles. Elevate your Chinese cuisine experience in just 15–20 minutes!

If you are using dried fermented black beans, place them in a small bowl and rinse under warm water. Drain and crush the beans using your fingers.

Place all the ingredients, except the oil, in a bowl and massage into the chicken. Once all the ingredients are well mixed, add the oil and massage again.

Now place the marinated chicken in a shallow, heatproof bowl and then in a steamer. Cook for 15–20 minutes, or until the chicken is tender and cooked all the way through.

Serve with rice or noodles as part of a fabulous authentic Chinese meal.

Chef's Tip

If you add the oil too early it will create a barrier and the meat will not be able to absorb the other ingredients.

CANTONESE CRISPY SPRING ONION CHICKEN

Succulent chicken legs enriched with fragrant ginger, garlic and spring onions (scallions). Simmered in a rich Cantonese gravy, this quick and easy dish serves four and promises a delightful taste experience in just 25 minutes. Serve it up and savour the goodness!

Serves 4

Preparation time: 5 minutes

Cooking time: 25 minutes

2 tbsp vegetable oil

4 skin-on, bone-in chicken leg quarters

3 slices of ginger

3 garlic cloves, roughly chopped

Bunch of spring onions (scallions), finely chopped (greens and whites separated)

For the sauce

2 tbsp oyster sauce

1 tbsp light soy sauce

2 tsp dark soy sauce

1¼ tbsp chicken powder

750ml (3 cups) water

2 tbsp Chinese rice wine (Shaoxing wine)

2 tsp cornflour (cornstarch), mixed with 4 tsp water

Add the oil to a wok over a medium-high heat, then add the chicken legs, skin-side down, and fry until golden brown. Turn the legs over and brown the other side. Once both sides are golden, add the ginger and garlic and fry until fragrant. Add the spring onion whites and cook for a further 1–2 minutes.

In a bowl, combine all the sauce ingredients, except the cornflour mixture. Mix well, then pour into the wok and slowly bring to the boil. Place a lid on the wok, reduce the heat to a simmer and cook for a further 15 minutes or until the chicken is tender and cooked all the way through.

Once the chicken is cooked, remove the legs and then give the sauce a good mix. If the sauce has nearly all evaporated, you can add more water. Return to the boil and stir in your cornflour mixture to thicken.

Place the chicken on a serving plate, pour over the Cantonese gravy and scatter over the spring onion greens to serve.

CHILLI BEAN CHICKEN AND POTATOES

Serves 2

Preparation time: 8 minutes

Cooking time: 12 minutes

2 potatoes (use waxy potatoes if you can)

120ml (½ cup) vegetable oil

350g (12oz) skin-on, boneless chicken thighs

3 dried Thai red chillies, roughly chopped

3 garlic cloves, thinly sliced

5 spring onions (scallions), cut into 5cm (2in) lengths

1 onion, thinly sliced

1 tbsp doubanjiang

2 tsp light soy sauce

½ tbsp oyster sauce

1 tsp sugar

Ready in less than 20 minutes, this spicy and satisfying dish features tender chicken, crispy potatoes and a fiery chilli bean kick. A speedy culinary adventure awaits!

Begin by slicing the potatoes into thin rounds, then soak in water for 5 minutes to remove any excess starch. Drain and dry thoroughly. Heat the oil in a saucepan and fry the potatoes until lightly browned and tender. Drain and set the potatoes to one side.

Cut the chicken thighs into thin strips and, using some of the leftover oil from frying the potatoes, fry the chicken until golden brown. Add the dried chillies and garlic and fry over a medium heat for a few minutes. Now add the spring onions and onion and fry until translucent. Add the remaining ingredients and, once combined, add the cooked potatoes and toss in the sauce.

Transfer to serving plates and enjoy.

EXPRESS CHICKEN CURRY

Serves 2

Preparation time: 5 minutes

Cooking time: 15 minutes

300g (10½oz) skin-on, boneless chicken thighs
1 tbsp minced ginger
2 tbsp minced garlic
1 tbsp fish sauce
2 tbsp curry powder
2 tbsp vegetable oil
1 small red onion, finely sliced
6 fresh curry leaves
125g (½ cup) coconut cream (coconut cream is thicker than coconut milk)
Salt, to taste

Enjoy the exotic flavours of succulent chicken marinated in ginger, garlic and curry powder, simmered to perfection in a savoury coconut cream sauce. Ready in minutes!

Cut the chicken into bite-sized pieces, place in a bowl and add the ginger, garlic, fish sauce and curry powder. Mix well and set to one side.

Place a wok over a medium heat, add the oil and gently soften the onion until tender and translucent. Add the chicken, increase the heat to medium-high and brown the chicken all over.

Once the chicken is partially cooked and browned, add 500ml (2 cups) of water and the curry leaves and give everything a really good mix. Reduce the heat and simmer for 5 minutes. Finally, add the coconut cream, stir and continue to cook until slightly thickened. Check for seasoning and adjust with salt to your preference.

FIERY CHILLI CHICKEN AND BEANSPROUT SALAD

Serves 4

Preparation time: 8 minutes

Cooking time: 6 minutes

450g (1lb) chicken breasts, thinly sliced

300g (10½oz) beansprouts

For the marinade

1 tbsp oyster sauce

2 tsp rice vinegar

1 tsp dark soy sauce

2 tsp light soy sauce

1 tbsp Chinese rice wine (Shaoxing wine)

½ tbsp cornflour (cornstarch)

1 tbsp vegetable oil

For the sauce

1 tbsp minced garlic

2 tsp chilli powder of your choice

2 red chillies, finely chopped

2 spring onions (scallions), finely chopped

2 tbsp vegetable oil

1 tbsp oyster sauce

1 tbsp light soy sauce

1 tsp chicken powder

1 tbsp toasted sesame seeds

Enjoy the explosive flavours of this fiery chicken salad – thinly sliced and marinated juicy chicken meets the scorching embrace of red chillies and aromatic spices. Combined with the fresh crunch of beansprouts, this salad delivers a multi-sensory experience with every bite.

Place the sliced chicken and all the marinade ingredients, except the oil, in a bowl and massage them into the meat. Once combined, add the oil and gently massage again. Set to one side for a couple of minutes while you prepare the sauce.

In a heatproof bowl, add the garlic, chilli powder, red chillies and spring onions. In a small saucepan, heat the oil to boiling and carefully pour over the mixture so everything sizzles. Mix well, then add the remaining sauce ingredients and combine.

Heat a saucepan of water over a medium-high heat, add the chicken and cook for 3–5 minutes, or until the chicken is tender and cooked all the way through. Drain and allow to rest while you steep the beansprouts.

Place the beansprouts in a bowl and pour over boiling water, steep for 30 seconds and then drain.

Now place the cooked chicken, beansprouts and sauce in a serving bowl and gently combine to serve.

GINGER GARLIC HOISIN-GLAZED CHICKEN

Serves 2

Preparation time: 10 minutes

Cooking time: 20 minutes

2 skin-on, boneless chicken legs
3 garlic cloves, minced
1 tbsp minced ginger
3 tbsp hoisin sauce
2 tbsp vegetable oil
1 tbsp honey

Succulent, deboned chicken legs are marinated in a rich blend of garlic, ginger, hoisin sauce and honey. A quick stir-fry results in a sticky and savoury glaze, making this dish a true delight for your taste buds.

Place the chicken in a large bowl along with the garlic, ginger, hoisin sauce and 2 tablespoons of water, then massage the marinade ingredients into the meat and set to one side.

Heat a wok over a medium-high heat and add the oil. Once hot, add the chicken skin-side down and fry until golden. Turn the chicken over and continue to cook until the flesh is golden brown. Now pour in the remaining marinade along with 3 tablespoons of water, reduce the heat to low and simmer, covered, for 10 minutes. Remove the lid, drizzle over the honey and stir in. Once the sauce has reduced and thickened, remove the chicken, chop into bite-sized pieces and arrange on a serving plate. Pour over the remaining sauce and enjoy with fresh steamed rice or noodles.

SWEET SPRING ONION ROAST CHICKEN LEGS

Serves 2–4

Preparation time: 5 minutes, plus 20 minutes marinating

Cooking time: 30 minutes

- 6–8 chicken drumsticks
- Thumb-sized piece of ginger, cut into matchsticks
- 2 tbsp Chinese rice wine (Shaoxing wine)
- 1 tbsp light soy sauce
- ½ tbsp dark soy sauce
- 1 tbsp honey
- 2 tbsp oyster sauce
- 2 tsp chicken powder
- Bunch of spring onions (scallions), cut into 5cm (2in) lengths
- 2–3 tbsp vegetable oil

Marinated in a flavourful blend of ginger, soy sauce, honey and more, these succulent drumsticks are gently roasted on a bed of aromatic spring onions (scallions). A quick and easy dish for any occasion.

Begin by cutting three slits into your drumsticks, top to bottom and to the bone. This will speed up the cooking process and allow the marinade to tenderize the meat.

Place the drumsticks in a bowl along with the remaining ingredients, except the spring onions and oil, and, using your hands, massage the marinade into your chicken, ensuring everything is well mixed. Allow to marinate for 20 minutes.

Line an air-fryer basket with parchment paper or foil, then place the spring onions into the basket, creating a spring onion bed. Place the drumsticks on top. Using a brush, cover each drumstick with oil (or you could use a good spray oil).

Cook at 180°C (350°F) for 25 minutes, checking halfway through and turning the drumsticks over for even cooking.

If you do not have an air fryer, you can cook them in an oven at the same temperature, turning the drumsticks over at the halfway point.

Serve in the centre of the table with bowls of freshly steamed rice.

GINGER SOY CHICKEN

Serves 2–4

Preparation time: 5 minutes, plus 20 minutes marinating

Cooking time: 10 minutes

450g (1lb) boneless, skinless chicken thighs, cut into 2.5cm (1in) cubes

1 Chinese lap cheong sausage, thinly sliced

For the marinade

1 tbsp oyster sauce

1 tbsp Chinese rice wine (Shaoxing wine)

½ tbsp Chinese rice vinegar

Pinch of white pepper

2 tsp cornflour (cornstarch)

For the sauce

1 tbsp vegetable oil

6–8 slices of peeled ginger (about 75g/2½oz)

2 garlic cloves, minced

2 tbsp light soy sauce

2 tbsp Chinese rice wine (Shaoxing wine)

2 tbsp oyster sauce

1 tbsp sugar

3 spring onions (scallions), chopped into 5cm (2in) lengths and bruised

Tender, marinated chicken thighs infused with Chinese sausage, oyster sauce and rice wine. Quick and easy to prepare, this aromatic dish serves 2–4 hungry diners and pairs perfectly with steamed rice. Enjoy classic Cantonese flavours in just 10 minutes of cooking!

Begin by placing the chicken in a bowl along with all the marinade ingredients, then massage them into the meat and set to one side for 20 minutes.

Place a wok over a medium-high heat, add the oil and, once hot, add the ginger and fry until fragrant. Then add the garlic, quickly followed by the marinated chicken and sausage. Fry until the chicken has begun to brown, then add the soy sauce, rice wine, oyster sauce and sugar. Stir to combine and then add spring onions. Reduce the heat to a simmer and continue to cook for a further 2–3 minutes.

Serve over freshly steamed rice.

LEMONGRASS CHICKEN

Serves 4

Preparation time: 10 minutes, plus 30 minutes marinating

Cooking time: 15 minutes

450–600g (1–1lb 5oz) boneless, skin-on chicken thighs, cut into 3cm (1¼in) chunks

3 tbsp lemongrass paste

3 tbsp fish sauce

2 tbsp light soy sauce

Juice of 2 limes

3 tbsp grated garlic

2 tbsp brown rice syrup (or maple syrup)

3 spring onions (scallions), finely chopped

2 tbsp vegetable oil

Elevate your taste buds with this succulent chicken, marinated in a harmonious blend of lemongrass, fish sauce and zesty lime. These skewers deliver a burst of Thai-inspired flavour, with my unique take.

Combine all the ingredients, except the oil, in a large bowl and massage the marinade into the chopped chicken. Set to one side to marinate for 30 minutes. After 30 minutes, add the oil and mix well.

Evenly thread the marinated chicken on to skewers (metal or wooden work equally well here).

Preheat the grill (broiler) or a barbecue and, once hot, cook the chicken skewers for 12–15 minutes, remembering to turn them frequently for even cooking and to prevent burning.

Serve with noodles, rice or with a crunchy salad.

SWEET GARLIC CHICKEN

Serves 2

Preparation time: 5 minutes

Cooking time: 15 minutes

350g (12oz) skin-on, boneless chicken thighs

1 tbsp oyster sauce

60g (½ cup) cornflour (cornstarch)

4 tbsp vegetable oil

For the sauce

2 tbsp butter

1 garlic bulb, peeled and roughly chopped

3 tbsp light soy sauce

1 tbsp mirin

90g (¼ cup) honey

Speedy, succulent chicken, marinated and fried to perfection, coated in a delectable, sweet garlic sauce. An irresistible meal in just 20 minutes.

Place the chicken thighs in a bowl, add the oyster sauce and massage it into the chicken. Now dredge the chicken in the cornflour and shake off the excess. Place a wok over a medium heat, add the oil and fry the chicken until golden brown and cooked all the way through, remembering to turn it frequently for even cooking.

Once the chicken is cooked, remove it from the wok, add the butter, then gently fry the garlic, stirring frequently as it can burn easily. Once the garlic has turned a light golden brown, add the soy sauce, mirin and honey. Once hot, add the chicken and cook for a further 1–2 minutes.

Cut the chicken into bite-sized slices and serve over freshly steamed sticky white rice with your favourite vegetable sides.

SICHUAN VELVETED CHICKEN WITH PEANUTS

Serves 2

Preparation time: 5 minutes

Cooking time: 10 minutes

350g (12oz) chicken breasts, cut into 1cm (½in) cubes

120ml (½ cup) vegetable oil

1 tsp Sichuan peppercorns

3 spring onions (scallions), finely chopped (whites and greens separated)

2 red chillies, finely chopped

160g (¼ cup) roasted peanuts

For the velveting

½ tsp salt

Pinch of white pepper

1 tbsp Chinese rice wine (Shaoxing wine)

1 tsp dark soy sauce

1 egg white

2 tsp cornflour (cornstarch)

1 tbsp vegetable oil

For the sauce

1½ tsp cornflour (cornstarch)

1½ tbsp light soy sauce

½ tbsp sugar

1½ tbsp Chinese black vinegar

Tender chicken cubes, coated in a velvety egg white mixture, stir-fried with Sichuan peppercorns, red chilli and black vinegar, then crowned with roasted peanuts. A symphony of spicy, nutty goodness.

Place the chicken in a bowl along with all the velveting ingredients, except the oil. Massage the ingredients into the chicken. Once combined, add the oil and massage into the chicken.

Place a wok over a medium heat, add the 120ml (½ cup) of vegetable oil and, once hot, add the chicken and gently fry until lightly browned. Drain the chicken and set to one side.

Combine all the sauce ingredients in a bowl, mixing well.

Return the wok to a medium heat along with a little of the leftover oil from frying, add the Sichuan peppercorns and toast until fragrant. Then add the spring onion whites and the red chillies and fry for a few seconds. Now add the cooked chicken and the sauce, stir well and gently bring to the boil. Once the sauce has reached a gentle boil, remove from the heat, add the peanuts and stir through.

Transfer to a serving plate and top with the spring onion greens.

SICHUAN-STYLE GARLIC BUTTER PRAWNS WITH SAUTÉED ONIONS AND PEPPERS

Serves 2–4

Preparation time: 5 minutes

Cooking time: 16 minutes

12–16 tiger prawns (shrimp)
3 tbsp butter
1 tbsp olive oil
1 large Spanish onion, finely diced
7 garlic cloves, finely chopped
½ green (bell) pepper, finely diced
½ red (bell) pepper, finely diced
1 red chilli, finely diced
2 tsp chicken powder
Pinch of white pepper
Pinch of salt (optional)
2 tsp cornflour (cornstarch), mixed with 4 tsp water

Enjoy the rich taste of Sichuan cuisine with these succulent tiger prawns (shrimp), sautéed with aromatic onion, garlic and colourful (bell) peppers. A mouthwatering delight cooked in just 16 minutes.

Many Chinese people love to cook tiger prawns whole, so if you'd like to give this a go, then here is how to prepare them. If, like many, you prefer your prawns peeled, begin by removing the head and then gently wiggle the tail and this should come away with the prawn intact. Now peel the remainder of the legs and shell from the body of the prawn but please keep all of the shells and heads as they can be used to make a wonderful fish stock. Now, using a very sharp knife, cut a slit along the back of the prawn to remove the digestive tract. Rinse the prawns under cold water and drain.

In a wok over a medium-low heat, add the butter and oil and gently sauté the onion and garlic for 8–10 minutes. Once the garlic and onion are translucent, buttery and super soft, increase the heat to medium-high, then add the prawns and cook for 2–3 minutes. Once the prawns are a lovely pink colour, add the peppers and diced chilli and give everything a good mix. Sprinkle in the chicken powder and white pepper and pour in 240ml (1 cup) of water. Bring the sauce to a gentle boil, check the seasoning and add the salt if required. Give the cornflour mixture a stir to loosen and slowly pour into the sauce, stirring at the same time. Turn off the heat and serve the delicious garlicky tiger prawns over steamed rice with a side of fresh Chinese greens.

FRIED CHICKEN

Serves 2–4

Preparation time: 10 minutes, plus 20 minutes marinating

Cooking time: 12 minutes

500g (1lb 2oz) boneless, skin-on chicken thighs, cut into bite-sized chunks

700ml (3 cups) vegetable oil

For the marinade

1 tbsp light soy sauce

2 tsp dark soy sauce

2 tbsp sake or Chinese rice wine (Shaoxing wine)

1 tbsp sesame oil

1 tsp salt

Pinch of white pepper

2 tbsp garlic paste

1 tbsp ginger paste

3 tbsp cornflour (cornstarch), plus 125g (1 cup) for dredging

For the sriracha mayo

100ml (½ cup) Japanese kewpie mayonnaise (or you can use normal mayo)

3 tbsp sriracha sauce

1 tbsp garlic paste

Pinch of salt

Pinch of ground black pepper

1 tbsp rice vinegar

Fried chicken is well-loved throughout East and Southeast Asia, each version using a different batter and base flavours. Karaage chicken is a famous example of a Japanese Chinese dish, originating in a Chinese restaurant in Japan. It was also influenced by cooking methods brought to Japan by Portuguese missionaries, such as frying. Here's my take on this scrumptious chicken: it's crispy on the outside and tender on the inside. Marinated in a heavenly blend of soy sauce, sake and aromatic spices, these chicken bites are double-fried to crisp perfection.

Place the chopped chicken and all the marinade ingredients, except the cornflour for dredging, in a bowl and massage the ingredients together using your hand. This will help to tenderize the meat. Set to one side for at least 20 minutes, or for a couple of hours if you have time.

In a clean bowl, combine the sriracha mayo ingredients and mix well. Place in the fridge to keep cool.

Dredge the marinated chicken in the extra cornflour, shake off any extra and place on a wire rack while you repeat with the remaining chicken.

In a deep-sided pan, heat the oil to 180°C (350°F) and carefully fry the chicken in batches for 5–6 minutes, or until golden brown, and drain on paper towels or a wire rack. Increase the heat and bring the oil up to 200°C (400°F), then fry the chicken for a second time for 1–2 minutes, or until crispy. Drain and serve with the sriracha mayo.

Great for snacking or as part of a main meal.

VELVETED CHILLI PEPPER CHICKEN

Serves 2

Preparation time: 5 minutes

Cooking time: 8 minutes

- 350g (12oz) chicken breasts, cut into thin slices across the grain
- 1 tbsp minced garlic
- 2 spring onions (scallions), finely chopped
- 220g (1 cup) red and green chillies, diagonally cut into bite-sized pieces

For the velveting

- 1 tbsp Chinese rice wine (Shaoxing wine)
- 1 tbsp oyster sauce
- 1 tsp dark soy sauce
- 2 tsp cornflour (cornstarch)
- 3 tbsp vegetable oil

Get ready for a fiery feast. Thin slices of chicken are velveted for silky tenderness and stir-fried with a medley of red and green chillies, garlic and spring onions (scallions). Spice lovers, this one's for you!

Place the chicken in a bowl along with all the velveting ingredients, except the oil. Massage the velveting ingredients into the chicken. Once combined, add 1 tablespoon of the oil and massage it into the chicken.

Place a wok over a medium heat, along with the remaining oil. Once hot, add the chicken and gently fry until lightly browned. Add the garlic and spring onions and continue to fry for a further 45 seconds, or until fragrant. Finally, add the chillies, combine well and, once the air is aromatic and spicy, transfer to serving plates.

beef and pork

GRIDDLED SOY GINGER CHILLI RIBS

These succulent pork ribs are marinated in a tantalizing mixture of Chinese rice beer, soy sauce, miso paste and aromatic spices. After a tenderizing steam bath, they hit the griddle for a sizzling finish, resulting in a dish that's both tender and sticky with a gentle chilli kick.

Serves 2

Preparation time: 10 minutes, plus 40 minutes marinating and tenderizing

Cooking time: 50 minutes

600g (1lb 5oz) pork ribs

1 tsp salt

2 tbsp rice vinegar

3 tbsp vegetable oil

For the marinade

100ml (scant ½ cup) Chinese rice beer

100ml (scant ½ cup) light soy sauce

1 tbsp chilli powder of your choice

2 tbsp miso paste

1 tbsp sesame oil

2 tbsp honey

2 tbsp garlic paste

1 tbsp ginger paste

Begin by placing the ribs in a large bowl along with the salt, rice vinegar and enough water to cover them. Give the ribs a good wash and allow them to sit for 20 minutes in the water. This process will not only tenderize the meat but also remove any impurities. After 20 minutes, drain, then rinse and drain again.

In another bowl, mix all the marinade ingredients together well, then separate one third of the marinade and set to one side. Add the rinsed and dried ribs to the larger bowl of marinade and marinate for a further 20 minutes.

Place the marinated ribs in a steamer basket and steam for 30 minutes until tender. Remove from the steamer and allow to cool.

Place a griddle pan over a medium-high heat, add the oil to the ribs and massage into the meat. Place the ribs on the hot griddle and baste with the reserved marinade – continue this process every couple of minutes. Once the ribs have a thick, sticky glaze and are heated all the way through, they are ready to serve.

SALT AND PEPPER PORK CHOPS

Serves 2

Preparation time: 10 minutes

Cooking time: 25 minutes

2 large or 4 small pork chops, rind on

2 tbsp vegetable oil

1 small onion, finely diced

1 small red (bell) pepper, finely diced

2 garlic cloves, sliced

½ tsp sea salt flakes

½ tsp ground black pepper

For the marinade

2 tbsp light soy sauce

1 tbsp Chinese five spice

1 tbsp red wine or dry sherry

1–2 tbsp cornflour (cornstarch)

2–3 tbsp vegetable oil

A revered dish in East Asian cooking, this culinary gem masterfully blends the robust flavours of salt and pepper to elevate humble pork chops. Uncover the secret to achieving tender, succulent meat while delving into a regional love affair with this timeless combination of ingredients.

Begin by cutting slits into the pork rind, which will help it render as it cooks. Next, using a sharp knife (to release any tension from the day), stab the meat all over. Lastly, using a tenderizer or heavy rolling pin, beat the pork chops. This process will help shorten and break the muscle fibres to ensure tender pieces of meat once cooked (while leaving you in a completely zen state to prepare the rest of the dish).

Place the chops in a large bowl and add all the marinade ingredients except the oil, as this creates a barrier and prevents the pork from absorbing the other flavours. Massage the marinade into the pork, then finally add the oil and ensure each chop is coated evenly.

Preheat an air fryer or the oven to 190°C/375°F/Gas 5. Place the pork on a wire rack in the air fryer or oven and cook for 12–15 minutes. Then turn over the pork chops, increase the heat to 200°C/400°F/Gas 6 and cook for a further 8–10 minutes. Once cooked, place on a wire rack to cool slightly.

Place a frying pan (skillet) or wok over a medium-high heat, add the oil along with the diced onion, red pepper and garlic and fry until fragrant. Evenly sprinkle in the salt and pepper, then toss in the pork chops to coat in the seasoning and serve hot.

SPICY CHINESE SEOUL-FOOD HOT-DOG STIR-FRY

Serves 2

Preparation time: 10 minutes

Cooking time: 6 minutes

2 tbsp vegetable oil

2 garlic cloves, minced

300g (10½oz) American-style hot dogs (franks), cut into bite-sized pieces

1 small onion, cubed

350g (2 cups) mixed (bell) peppers, cubed

1 carrot, peeled and sliced into bite-sized pieces

2 tbsp gochujang

1 tbsp tomato ketchup

2 tbsp honey

2 tbsp water

2 tsp sesame oil

1 tbsp toasted sesame seeds

This dish embodies the spirit of modern fusion cuisine by blending elements from American, Korean, and Chinese culinary traditions. The foundation of the dish – stir-frying – is quintessentially Chinese, a technique used to ensure that the flavours remain sharp and distinct.

Place a wok over a medium-high heat and add the oil along with the garlic and fry until fragrant. Add the chopped hot dogs and stir. Now add the onion and cook for 2–3 minutes until translucent. Add the mixed peppers and carrot, toss to combine, then add the gochujang, tomato ketchup, honey and water. Your vegetables should be crispy and colourful so don't overcook them. Transfer to a serving plate and drizzle with the sesame oil and sprinkle with the toasted sesame seeds.

ROLLED SPAM RICE ROLLS

Serves 2–4

Preparation time: 10 minutes

Cooking time: 20 minutes

300g (1⅓ cups) sushi rice

1 x 340g (11¾oz) can of Spam

2 tbsp toasted sesame seeds

1 tbsp sesame oil

½ tsp salt

5 sheets of nori, chopped into 8–10cm (3¼–4in) squares

Spam rice rolls offer a delectable fusion of flavours and a nod to the enduring love for Spam in East Asian cuisine. Delicately seasoned sushi rice envelops savoury Spam, creating irresistible bite-sized rolls. A heartily moreish snack or side!

Wash the rice under warm water until the water runs clear – this normally takes 3–4 rinses. Place the rice into a rice cooker or saucepan. Add enough water so it sits about 2cm (¾in) above the top of the rice. Turn the rice cooker on and put on the lid. If you are boiling the rice, cook in a saucepan over a medium-high heat until all the water has been absorbed. Switch off the heat and cover with a tight lid. Now leave it alone for 15 minutes.

While the rice is cooking, cut the Spam into flat tiles and fry without any oil until golden brown. Remove from the pan, cut the Spam into sticks and set to one side.

Once the rice is cooked and rested, stir it to loosen the grains and add the sesame seeds, sesame oil and salt for seasoning. Mix well.

Take a square of nori and spread on enough rice so it covers the sheet and is about 1–2 grains thick. Add a row of Spam and roll into a cylinder. Repeat until all the mixture has been used, then place the rolls on a serving plate and enjoy as part of your meal or as a snack.

SUCCULENT FIVE-SPICE BEEF FLANK

Serves 2–4

Preparation time: 10 minutes, plus 20 minutes marinating

Cooking time: 15 minutes

- 450g (1lb) beef flank, sliced against the grain and cut into 5mm (¼in) cubes
- 2 tbsp oyster sauce
- 3 tsp Chinese five spice
- 3 tbsp cornflour (cornstarch)
- 2 tbsp vegetable oil
- 2 tbsp finely chopped garlic
- 2 tsp finely chopped ginger
- 120ml (½ cup) light soy sauce
- 120ml (½ cup) water
- 200g (7oz) soft brown sugar
- ½ tsp sesame oil
- 5 spring onions (scallions), finely chopped

Tender beef flank, marinated in a rich and aromatic blend of oyster sauce and Chinese five spice, delivers a mouthwatering dish that delights with every bite. It's heaped with spring onions (scallions) for a flavourful finishing touch.

Place the beef in a large bowl along with the oyster sauce, Chinese five spice and cornflour, then massage into the meat and place to one side for at least 20 minutes.

Heat a wok over a medium-high heat, add the oil and, once hot, brown the beef on all sides. Once the beef has browned, reduce the heat down to medium and then add the garlic and ginger and cook until fragrant. Now add the soy sauce, water and sugar. Bring to the boil and then reduce the heat to a simmer. Cook for a few more minutes until the sauce has thickened. Transfer to serving plates and top with the chopped spring onions.

SWEET VINEGAR RIBS

Serves 2–4

Preparation time: 30 minutes

Cooking time: 25 minutes

450–600g (1lb–1lb 5oz) pork ribs, separated into individual ribs and cut into 5cm (2in) pieces

60ml (¼ cup) white rice vinegar, plus 1 tbsp

1 tsp salt

3 tbsp vegetable oil

3–4 slices of ginger

2 star anise

3 spring onions (scallions), chopped into 5cm (2in) lengths (whites and greens separated)

3 tbsp sugar

2 tbsp oyster sauce

1 tbsp light soy sauce

3 Chinese dried plums, stoned

60ml (¼ cup) water

½ tbsp dark soy sauce

For the marinade

½ tsp salt

2 tbsp light soy sauce

¼ tsp white pepper

2 tbsp Chinese rice wine (Shaoxing wine) or dry sherry

1 tbsp cornflour (cornstarch)

1 tbsp vegetable oil

Delve into the delightful flavours of my sweet vinegar ribs, where you'll savour succulent, tender pork ribs bathed in a sweet yet tangy sauce. The combination of rice vinegar, soy sauce and aromatic spices creates a harmonious blend that's sure to please your palate. Enjoy this delicious dish with family and friends.

Place the ribs in a large bowl, add just enough water to cover them, then add the 1 tablespoon of vinegar and the salt and give everything a really good mix. Allow to soak for 15 minutes – this will help tenderize the meat and also remove any impurities. Drain and set to one side.

Once the ribs are dry, add all the marinade ingredients except the oil. Massage the marinade into the ribs and, once covered, add the oil, massage again and leave to sit for a further 10–15 minutes.

Place a wok over a medium heat and fry the ribs in the oil until golden brown, turning to ensure even cooking. Once browned, remove the ribs from the wok and set to one side. Then fry the ginger, star anise and spring onion whites in the wok until aromatic. Add the sugar and continue to fry until the sugar has melted. Return the ribs to the wok and stir to combine. Now add all the remaining ingredients, except the spring onion greens. Bring to the boil, then reduce the heat to low and simmer for 5–10 minutes, or until the ribs are tender and the sauce has thickened.

Transfer to a serving plate and sprinkle over the spring onion greens to garnish.

CANTONESE STEAMED PORK

Serves 4

Preparation time: 10 minutes

Cooking time: 16–18 minutes

500g (1lb 2oz) pork belly, skin removed

1 tbsp oyster sauce

1 tbsp Chinese rice wine (Shaoxing wine)

2 tsp light soy sauce

2 tsp fish sauce

1 tsp sugar

2 tsp chicken powder

Pinch of white pepper

65g (2¼oz) carrot, peeled and finely diced

180g (6oz) water chestnuts, finely diced

3 spring onions (scallions), finely chopped (greens and whites separated)

1 tbsp cornflour (cornstarch)

4 tbsp water

1 tsp vegetable oil

3 slices of ginger

This savoury dish features tender pork belly, crunchy water chestnuts and aromatic spices, all expertly combined and perfectly steamed. It's a taste of Cantonese cuisine you won't want to miss.

Slice the belly pork into thin strips, then into matchsticks and then into small dice. Once you have small dice, run your knife through the mixture a couple of times. You want quite a coarse mince.

Now add the oyster sauce, rice wine, soy sauce, fish sauce, sugar, chicken powder and white pepper to the pork. Mix well to combine all the ingredients. Add the diced carrot, water chestnuts and spring onion whites and combine into the mixture. Now add the cornflour – this is where you need to get your hands in and really massage the mixture together to make it sticky. Once sticky, add 1 tablespoon of the water and repeat until you have added all the water and it has been absorbed into the pork mixture.

Now rub the oil onto a high-lipped plate and then flatten out the pork mixture on the plate to make one large disc. Lay the slices of ginger on top and place the plate into a steamer for 16–18 minutes, depending on the fattiness of your pork. Once the pork is cooked, remove the plate from the steamer and place on the table. Sprinkle with the spring onion greens to serve.

This dish is delicious served with freshly steamed rice.

STUFFED FRIED TOFU

Serves 2–4

Preparation time: 15 minutes

Cooking time: 12 minutes

- 3 Chinese dried mushrooms (optional)
- 200g (7oz) minced (ground) pork
- 3 garlic cloves, minced
- 1 tsp chicken powder
- 1 tbsp oyster sauce
- 1 tsp salt
- 2 tsp sugar
- 2 tsp cornflour (cornstarch)
- ¼ tsp white pepper
- 5 spring onions (scallions), finely chopped (greens and whites separated)
- 12 pieces of pre-fried tofu (3–4cm/1¼–1½in cubes)
- 2 tbsp vegetable oil

For the sauce

- 160ml (⅔ cup) water
- 2 tbsp oyster sauce
- 1 tbsp light soy sauce
- ½ tsp dark soy sauce
- 2 tsp cornflour (cornstarch)

Bite-sized tofu cubes filled with a savoury mixture of minced (ground) pork, Chinese mushrooms and aromatic seasonings. Delicate yet satisfying.

Begin by soaking the Chinese mushrooms in boiling water, if using. Once fully rehydrated squeeze out the excess water and finely chop.

Combine all the remaining ingredients, except the tofu, spring onion greens and oil, and mix well – the mixture should be slightly sticky when combined. If needed you can add a little more cornflour to make it stickier.

Now, carefully using a sharp pointed knife, cut a hollow into each tofu cube. Then, using a teaspoon, fill each hollow with the minced pork mixture. Repeat until all the mixture has been used, then set the tofu to one side.

Now combine all the sauce ingredients, ensuring you stir them well to dissolve the cornflour.

Place a wok over a medium-high heat, then add the oil and, once hot, add the tofu pieces, meat-side down. Cook for 3–4 minutes, or until golden brown, then using tongs or chopsticks, flip the tofu pieces over. Give the sauce a good stir to loosen the cornflour that may have settled at the bottom and pour over the tofu. Place a lid on the wok, reduce the heat to low and cook for 8–10 minutes. Finally, give the tofu a gentle stir, being careful not to break apart the filled pieces, then transfer to serving plates and top with the spring onion greens.

HOISIN GLAZED PORK RIBS

Serves 2

Preparation time: 5 minutes

Cooking time: 50 minutes

450g (1lb) pork ribs, separated into individual ribs

1 tsp salt

½ onion

3 slices of ginger

3 spring onions (scallions), cut in half

For the sauce

3 tbsp vegetable oil

1 onion, sliced

1 tbsp light soy sauce

½ tbsp dark soy sauce

3 tbsp hoisin sauce

1 tbsp sugar

3 tbsp water

These succulent ribs are braised to perfection with ginger, onion and spring onions (scallions), then coated in a sweet and savoury hoisin sauce. A tantalizing dish that's both tender and richly glazed.

Place the ribs in a large saucepan, cover with cold water and place over a medium-high heat. As the water begins to boil, start to skim off any impurities that float to the surface. Once most of the impurities have been removed, add the salt, onion, sliced ginger and spring onions. Reduce the heat to a simmer, cover and cook for a further 35 minutes.

Drain the cooked ribs and set to one side to cool.

Heat a non-stick wok over a medium-high heat along with the oil, then add the cooled ribs and fry until golden brown, turning often. Once the ribs are golden brown all over, add the onion and cook until translucent. Add the remaining ingredients, carefully mix well and cook for 2–3 minutes. Transfer to a serving plate and enjoy.

UMAMI BEEF AND MUSHROOMS

Serves 2–4

Preparation time: 5 minutes, plus 20 minutes marinating

Cooking time: 15 minutes

- 450g (1lb) beef sirloin
- 60ml (¼ cup) light soy sauce
- 60ml (¼ cup) mirin
- Pinch of white pepper, to taste
- 2 tbsp Chinese rice wine (Shaoxing wine) or dry sherry
- 1 tbsp vegetable oil
- 2 tbsp butter
- 1 Spanish onion, finely diced
- 3 tbsp minced garlic
- 250g (9oz) mushrooms (I used a mixture of fresh shiitake and chestnut), quartered or chopped into medium-sized pieces
- 30g (¼ cup) plain (all-purpose) flour
- 240ml (1 cup) beef stock
- 200ml (scant 1 cup) double (heavy) cream

A savoury symphony of flavours, thin slices of marinated beef and a medley of mushrooms dance in a velvety cream sauce. Delicious served over noodles or rice.

The best way to really thinly slice the beef is to pop it into the freezer for 30 minutes, then slice it against the grain on a 45-degree angle with a really sharp knife while still half-frozen.

Place the sliced beef in a bowl along with the soy sauce, mirin, white pepper and rice wine. Gently massage the meat and set it to one side for 20–30 minutes.

Place a wok over a medium-high heat along with the oil, then add the beef. Once you've fanned out the beef in the wok, allow to sear and brown before flipping over. Once the beef has browned all over, remove from the pan and set to one side.

Place the same wok over a medium heat along with the butter, then add the onion and garlic and gently soften. At the same time, scrape the wok to help incorporate the meat juices that have clung to the bottom. Once the onion is tender and cooked through, add the mushrooms. After a minute or two, when the moisture from the onion has evaporated, sprinkle in the flour and stir to combine all the ingredients. Pour in the beef stock and as it comes to the boil keep stirring – the sauce will naturally thicken as you do this. Return the cooked beef to the sauce, mix well and then turn off the heat. Finally, slowly pour in the cream, continuing to stir. Serve over noodles or rice.

CRISPY PORK BELLY

Serves 2–4

Preparation time: 15 minutes

Cooking time: 55 minutes

450g (1lb) skin-on, flat piece of pork belly

2 tbsp Chinese rice wine (Shaoxing wine)

2 tbsp hoisin sauce

2 tsp Chinese five spice

2 tsp salt

2 tsp sugar, plus extra to serve

1 tsp white pepper

1–2 tbsp rice vinegar

100g (¾ cup) salt

1 egg white

1 tbsp vegetable oil

This recipe combines luscious pork belly with a symphony of flavours, from aromatic Chinese rice wine to rich, savoury hoisin sauce. The secret to the irresistible crunch of the crackling lies in the meticulous preparation and careful air-frying. Get ready to savour every bite of this exquisite dish.

Using paper towels, completely dry the pork belly. Then, using a metal skewer, puncture the skin of the pork with as many holes as possible – the more holes, the crispier the skin will be.

Flip the pork over and score the meat (cutting a third of the way through) with 5cm (2in) channels cut diagonally across the length of the meat. Mix the rice wine and hoisin sauce together and completely cover just the meat side in sauce, ensuring the sauce gets into the cuts. Now mix the five spice, 2 teaspoons of salt, the sugar and white pepper together and sprinkle this over the marinated meat and then massage it into all the nooks and crannies. Place the pork (meat-side down) on to a piece of foil, then fold the foil up around the sides of the pork, creating a tightly sealed tray. You do not want any of the meat visible, but the skin must remain uncovered. Now, using paper towels again, ensure the skin is completely dry, then brush with the rice vinegar. Mix the remaining salt with the egg white to make a salt paste and cover the skin with the mixture, ensuring no skin is visible.

Preheat an air fryer to 100°C (210°F), then add the pork and cook for 30 minutes. Remove the salt layer, dry the pork skin with paper towels again and then lightly brush with the oil. Increase the air-fryer temperature to 190°C (375°F), return the pork to the air fryer and cook for a further 25 minutes.

Remove the pork from the air fryer and allow to rest briefly before chopping into bite-sized chunks.

Alternatively, cook in an oven preheated to 180°C/350°F/Gas 4 for 45 minutes, then remove the salt crust and place back under a grill (broiler) on medium-high for roughly 15 minutes until puffed and crispy. Keep a close eye on the skin at this stage as it can burn quickly depending on the heat of the grill. Chop into bite-sized chunks.

Serve with a bowl of sugar to dip the pork into for a lip-smacking taste sensation.

CRISPY AUBERGINE PORK ROLLS

Serves 2–4

Preparation time: 12 minutes, plus 20 minutes resting

Cooking time: 7 minutes

For the filling

2 Japanese aubergines (eggplants)

220g (8oz) minced (ground) pork

3 spring onions (scallions), finely chopped

1 tbsp minced garlic

1 tbsp minced ginger

1 tbsp oyster sauce

½ tbsp Chinese rice wine (Shaoxing wine)

Pinch of salt

Pinch of white pepper

½ tbsp cornflour (cornstarch)

Vegetable oil, for frying

For the batter

125g (1 cup) plain (all-purpose) flour

30g (¼ cup) cornflour (cornstarch)

2 egg yolks

400ml (1¾ cups) iced water

Indulge in this delightful fusion of flavours with Japanese aubergine (eggplant) slices filled with a savoury blend of minced (ground) pork, spring onions (scallions), garlic, ginger and oyster sauce. Rolled into delectable cylinders, dipped in a light tempura batter and fried to a golden crisp, this quick-to-prepare, appetizing dish serves 2–4 and pairs perfectly with your favourite dipping sauce. Savour the crispy goodness!

Place all the filling ingredients in a bowl, except the aubergines, and mix well until the mixture becomes quite sticky. Cover with cling film (plastic wrap) and place in the fridge to rest.

In another bowl, mix the dry batter ingredients together. Whisk the egg yolks and then combine with the flour mixture and the iced water. Be careful not to overmix, so don't worry about any lumps in the mixture. Place the batter in the fridge while you assemble the rolls.

Using a vegetable peeler, cut long, thin strips of aubergine. Cover each aubergine strip in a thin layer of the pork mixture, then roll into a cylinder. Once all the pork mixture and aubergine strips have been used, heat about 7.5cm (3in) oil to 185°C (365°F) in a deep-sided pan.

Now dunk your aubergine rolls into the batter and carefully lower into the hot oil. Fry for 3–5 minutes, depending on how thick your rolls are, until golden brown and crispy.

Once cooked, drain and serve with your favourite dipping sauce. Sweet and sour and sweet chilli works really well with this recipe.

EASY CANTONESE ROAST PORK

Serves 2–4

Preparation time: 10 minutes, plus 20 minutes marinating

Cooking time: 50 minutes

2 x 150g (5½oz) pieces of pork shoulder

3 spring onions (scallions), roughly cut into 5cm (2in) lengths

3 slices of ginger

4 tbsp hoisin sauce

2 tbsp sugar

½ tbsp dark soy sauce

1 tbsp light soy sauce

1 tbsp oyster sauce

3 tbsp water

A Cantonese roast pork delight! This succulent pork shoulder is marinated in a flavourful mix of hoisin sauce, soy sauce and more, then air-fried to achieve a crispy exterior and tender interior. Savour it with steamed rice for a mouthwatering meal.

Begin by placing the pork in a bowl with all the remaining ingredients, then massage them into the pork. Leave it to marinate for at least 20 minutes.

Preheat an air fryer to 160°C (325°F). Place the pork in the air fryer, saving the remaining marinade, and air-fry for 20 minutes.

After 20 minutes, brush the pork with the remaining marinade, increase the temperature to 180°C (350°F) and cook for a further 30 minutes. Allow the cooked pork to rest for 15 minutes before carving and serving with freshly steamed rice.

If you don't have an air fryer, you can cook the pork in the oven at the same temperatures for the same length of time.

SWEET SOY FRIED PORK CHOPS

Perfectly golden, tender pork chops drizzled with my sweet soy sauce – a blend of light and dark soy sauces, oyster sauce and Chinese rice wine – for an irresistibly savoury-sweet finish.

Serves 2

Preparation time: 8 minutes

Cooking time: 10 minutes

400g (14oz) pork chops

For the marinade
1 tbsp oyster sauce
½ tbsp light soy sauce
½ tbsp Chinese rice wine (Shaoxing wine)
1½ tbsp cornflour (cornstarch)
Pinch of white pepper
½ tbsp vegetable oil, plus 1 tbsp for frying

For the sweet soy sauce
1 tbsp light soy sauce
½ tbsp dark soy sauce
1 tbsp oyster sauce
½ tbsp Chinese rice wine (Shaoxing wine)
2 tbsp water
2 tbsp sugar
1 tbsp vegetable oil

Begin by tenderizing the pork chops by beating them flat with a rolling pin, the back of a heavy knife or a meat tenderizer. Once the pork chops are nice and thin and tender, place them in a bowl along with all the marinade ingredients, except the oil. Massage the marinade into the meat, then add the oil and massage again to seal in the flavours.

Now make the sweet soy sauce. Place all the sauce ingredients in a saucepan and gently heat until the sugar has dissolved, then immediately remove from the heat and allow to cool.

Place a wok over a medium-high heat and fry the pork chops in the tablespoon of oil until golden brown, crispy and cooked all the way through. Once cooked, chop into slices and serve over freshly steamed rice along with the sweet soy sauce.

PORK BELLY CRUNCH

Serves: 4

Preparation time: 10 minutes, plus 2 hours marinating

Cooking time: 10–12 minutes

- 1 tbsp red miso paste
- 2 tbsp oyster sauce
- 2 tbsp Chinese rice wine (Shaoxing wine)
- 1 tbsp sugar
- 1 tbsp fish sauce
- 500g (1lb 2oz) skinless pork belly, cut into 3cm- (1¼in-) thick strips
- 2 tsp sesame oil
- 60g (½ cup) cornflour (cornstarch)
- 120ml (½ cup) vegetable oil

Irresistibly crispy and perfectly tender. Indulge in the crisp goodness of succulent pork belly strips, marinated to perfection, then fried to an enticing golden crunch.

Add the miso paste, oyster sauce, rice wine, sugar and fish sauce to a bowl and mix well. Massage the paste into the pork belly slices and once coated, set to one side to marinate for 2 hours.

Once the pork has marinated, drizzle over the sesame oil and carefully spread over the pork. Place the cornflour in a bowl and dredge each piece of pork in the flour until covered. Shake off any excess.

Heat the oil in a frying pan (skillet) or wok until it reaches about 180°C (350°F). Add the pork and fry until golden brown, crispy and cooked all the way through, remembering to flip over frequently for even cooking. Once cooked, drain, cut into bite-sized slices and serve.

HOT DOG SKEWERS

Serves 2

Preparation time: 8 minutes

Cooking time: 10 minutes

12 pieces of Korean-style rice cakes

6 hot dogs, (franks) cut in half

2 tbsp vegetable oil

For the sauce

2 tbsp sugar

1 tbsp tomato ketchup

1 tbsp brown sauce (I used A.1.)

1 tbsp light soy sauce

2 tsp sesame oil

½ tsp Chinese five spice

Modern Chinese cuisine has adapted and embraced ingredients and ideas from Western food traditions. In a similar vein, here I've fused hot dogs (franks) with traditionally Asian-style skewers. Skewering ingredients is a method seen in various Chinese dishes, notably in street foods such as lamb or chicken skewers (chuan'r) that are seasoned and grilled.

Begin by cooking the rice cakes and hot dogs in boiling water. Once they are tender, remove them both from the water and drain.

Place all the sauce ingredients in a saucepan, mix well and gently warm. Once the sauce is hot, turn off the heat.

Now thread 3 pieces of rice cake and 3 pieces of hot dog onto skewers, alternating the ingredients.

Place a wok over a medium heat, add the oil and fry the skewers for 5–6 minutes until they are lightly golden on both sides. Finally, coat each skewer with sauce and serve.

vegetables

CRISPY CHILLI AUBERGINE

Serves 2–4

Preparation time: 10 minutes

Cooking time: 15 minutes

For the fritters

- 2 aubergines (eggplants)
- 1 tsp salt
- 3 eggs
- 3 tbsp mayonnaise (use Japanese Kewpie mayo if you can)
- 60g (¼ cup) plain (all-purpose) flour
- 60g (½ cup) cornflour (cornstarch)
- Pinch of white pepper
- 1 tsp chilli powder of your choice
- 120ml (½ cup) vegetable oil

For the sauce

- 1 onion, thinly sliced
- 1 red (bell) pepper, sliced
- 1 carrot, peeled and cut into thin batons
- 2 tbsp minced garlic
- Pinch of salt
- 2 red chillies, finely chopped
- 3 tbsp white rice vinegar
- 2 tbsp tomato ketchup
- 60ml (¼ cup) water
- 3 tbsp hoisin sauce
- 3 tbsp sugar
- 1 tbsp cornflour (cornstarch), mixed with 2 tbsp water

Tender aubergine (eggplant) fingers fried to golden perfection, coated in a fiery yet sweet sauce, and served with a medley of colourful vegetables.

Peel the aubergines, then slice into 1.5cm- (⅝in-) thick slices, then into 1cm- (½in-) thick fingers. Place the slices into a saucepan of water along with the salt, then cover and poach for 5 minutes, or until just tender. Remove from the water and allow to drain.

Combine the eggs and mayonnaise, then mix well.

In a separate bowl, combine the flour, cornflour, white pepper and chilli powder and mix well.

Pour the oil into a wok or frying pan (skillet) over a medium heat and once it has reached 170–180°C (340–350°F), maintain this temperature.

Dredge each piece of poached aubergine in the flour mixture, then dip into the egg mixture. Shallow-fry in the oil until golden brown and super tender yet crispy on the outside. Drain and set to one side.

Place a wok over a medium-high heat with a little of the oil used to fry your aubergines. Add the onion, pepper and carrot and fry for 1–2 minutes until they become tender. Now add the garlic and, once fragrant, add the salt and mix well. Add the chopped chillies and remaining ingredients, except the cornflour mixture, and bring to the boil. Once boiling, add the cornflour mixture while stirring. Switch off the heat and then gently toss in the crispy aubergine.

Transfer to serving plates and enjoy.

CRISPY STICKY TOFU

Serves 2

Preparation time: 10 minutes

Cooking time: 20 minutes

1 x 300g (10½oz) block of firm tofu

60g (½ cup) cornflour (cornstarch)

3 tbsp vegetable oil

For the sauce

2 garlic cloves, minced

½ tbsp light soy sauce

2 tbsp sweet chilli sauce

½ tbsp rice vinegar

½ tbsp honey

2 tsp cornflour (cornstarch)

2 tbsp water

1 tbsp toasted sesame seeds

These golden nuggets of firm tofu are fried to perfection and coated in a sweet and savoury sauce, creating a sensational fusion of flavours and textures.

Begin by gently squeezing out any excess water from the tofu by pressing in a clean, dry dish towel.

Cut the tofu into even bite-sized pieces and dredge in the cornflour. Place a wok over a medium-high heat and, once hot, add the oil and fry the tofu until golden brown on all sides. Transfer to a plate and keep warm.

Combine all the sauce ingredients except the sesame seeds in the wok and heat. Once the sauce is hot and sticky, add the tofu and toss to coat each piece in the sauce. Transfer to serving plates and sprinkle with the toasted sesame seeds.

CRISPY SWEET POTATO BALLS

Serves 4

Preparation time: 8 minutes

Cooking time: 1 hour 10 minutes

450g (1lb) sweet potatoes

65g (⅓ cup) granulated sugar

220g (1¼ cups) glutinous rice flour

60g (½ cup) cornflour (cornstarch)

Vegetable oil, for frying

These golden orbs are made from tender sweet potatoes, sugar and glutinous rice flour, creating a delectable treat that's crispy on the outside and wonderfully sweet on the inside.

Preheat the oven to 200°C/400°F/Gas 6. Place the sweet potatoes on a tray and bake for 1 hour, or until tender. Remove and allow to cool for 15 minutes.

Remove and discard the skins from the sweet potatoes, then place the flesh into a large bowl, add the sugar and mash with a fork to combine completely.

In a large bowl, measure out the glutinous rice flour, then add the mashed sweet potato and knead to create a dough. Roll the mixture into a sausage shape and cut into 16 equal pieces. Roll each piece into a ball and then roll in the cornflour to lightly coat them. Gently shake off any excess.

In a deep-sided pan, heat the oil to 180°C (350°F) – you need enough oil for the balls to bob without touching the bottom of the pan. Carefully fry the sweet potato balls in batches until golden brown, crispy and cooked all the way through. Drain and serve as a snack or as part of a meal.

EASY FRIED TOFU

Serves 2

Preparation time: 5 minutes

Cooking time: 10 minutes

1 x 300g (10½oz) block of firm tofu

3 tbsp vegetable oil

5 spring onions (scallions), cut into 5cm (2in) lengths

1 tbsp garlic paste

For the sauce

½ tsp salt

2 tsp chicken powder or vegetable bouillon

1 tbsp light soy sauce

1 tsp dark soy sauce

1 tbsp Chinese black vinegar

1 tbsp oyster sauce

2 tbsp water

1 tbsp cornflour (cornstarch)

Indulge in the simple and savoury delights of crispy, golden tofu cubes, stir-fried with aromatic spring onions (scallions) and garlic, then coated in a flavourful sauce that's the perfect balance of salty and savoury. Enjoy this quick and satisfying dish as part of a classic Chinese meal.

Begin by gently squeezing out any excess water from the tofu by pressing it in a clean, dry dish towel.

Cut the tofu into even bite-sized pieces, then place a wok over a medium-high heat. Once hot, add the oil and fry the tofu until golden brown on all sides. Now add the spring onions and garlic and fry until fragrant.

Combine all the sauce ingredients, mix well and pour into the wok, gently combining with the tofu and coating each piece. Once the sauce has thickened and is coating the tofu, transfer to serving plates and enjoy.

GARLIC FRIED GREEN BEANS

Serves 2

Preparation time: 5 minutes

Cooking time: 8 minutes

120ml (½ cup) vegetable oil

350g (12oz) green beans, topped and tailed

6 garlic cloves, finely diced

Pinch of salt

2 tsp Chinese rice wine (Shaoxing wine)

1 tsp light soy sauce

Get ready to elevate your veggie game with these delectable green beans! Quick and easy to prepare, they're blistered and infused with aromatic garlic, making a sumptuous side dish.

Heat the oil in a wok over a medium heat and, once hot, fry the green beans in batches for about 30 seconds or until the skins blister. Drain on paper towels.

Carefully drain off the excess oil and, using what remains, place the wok back over a medium heat, then add the garlic and fry gently until aromatic. Now add the drained green beans and toss before adding the salt, rice wine and soy sauce. Mix well, then transfer to a serving plate and enjoy.

EGGCELLENT MAYO RAMEN DELIGHT

Serves 1–2

Preparation time: 2 minutes

Cooking time: 3 minutes

- 2 eggs
- 2 packets of ramen noodles (use your favourite)
- 3 spring onions (scallions), finely chopped
- 1 tbsp garlic paste
- 1 tsp ginger paste
- 2 tbsp Japanese Kewpie mayonnaise (or you can use normal mayo)
- 3 tbsp vegetable oil

This quick and easy ramen dish combines the creamy goodness of Kewpie mayo with aromatic garlic, ginger and spring onions (scallions). It's a savoury treat that's ready in just minutes. Perfect for a quick meal for one or to share with someone special.

In a bowl, add the eggs, ramen seasoning packets, chopped spring onions, garlic, ginger and mayonnaise and mix well.

In a small saucepan, heat the oil and, once hot, carefully and slowly stir into the seasoning mixture.

Cook the noodles in boiling water until tender, then drain and add to the seasoning mixture. Stir thoroughly and enjoy.

SPICY RICE CAKES

Serves 2–4

Preparation time: 30 minutes

Cooking time: 10 minutes

- 350g (12oz) Korean-style rice cakes
- 150–200g (5½–7oz) Chinese or Korean rice cakes, sliced
- 3 eggs
- 750ml (3¼ cups) fish stock OR 750ml water plus 1½ tbsp chicken powder or vegetable bouillon
- 2 tbsp gochujang
- 1 tbsp gochugaru
- 1 tbsp sugar
- 2 tbsp brown rice syrup (or you could use honey)
- 3 spring onions (scallions), cut into 5cm (2in) lengths

Rice cakes are ubiquitous in East Asian cuisines, though different in each one. I like to experiment with different versions, so here I give my take on Korean tteokbokki. Experience the fiery delight of spicy rice cakes soaked and simmered in a tantalizing fusion of gochujang, gochugaru and brown rice syrup. Alternatively, use doubanjiang (see page 14) instead of the gochujang for more of a fusion flavour. This mouthwatering meal is garnished with boiled eggs for a creamy, satisfying finish. A spicy, savoury treat perfect for breakfast or dinner.

Begin by soaking all the rice cakes in lukewarm water for 30 minutes, or following the packet instructions, while you prepare the remaining ingredients. Place the eggs in cold water and bring to the boil. Boil for 4–5 minutes, depending on the size of the eggs, drain and peel.

Once the rice cakes have soaked, drain and place them in a large saucepan along with the remaining ingredients, except the eggs. Slowly bring to the boil, mixing gently to ensure everything is well combined. Once the rice cakes are tender, turn off the heat, cut the eggs in half and place them on top of the rice cakes. This dish is best served piping hot.

Easy swaps

Brown rice syrup can be substituted with honey.

Gochugaru is becoming much more commonly available in supermarkets, but you can substitute it with sweet paprika in a pinch.

rice and noodles

SPICY SOBA NOODLES

Serves 2

Preparation time: 8 minutes

Cooking time: 3 minutes

300g (10½oz) dried soba noodles
200g (7oz) beansprouts

For the sauce
1 tbsp dried chilli flakes
3 spring onions (scallions), finely chopped
½ tbsp grated garlic
1 tbsp grated ginger
2 tbsp vegetable oil
2 tbsp light soy sauce
¾ tbsp dark soy sauce
3 tbsp smooth peanut butter
2 tbsp mirin
2 tbsp crushed roasted peanuts

Tender soba noodles and crisp beansprouts enveloped in a spicy, creamy, aromatic sauce. It's the perfect balance of heat and nuttiness, ready to tantalize your taste buds. Enjoy this quick and satisfying meal tonight!

Place the soba noodles in a saucepan of boiling water. Cook for 2–3 minutes until soft, then drain and set to one side. Meanwhile, place the beansprouts in a bowl and pour over boiling water, then leave for 1 minute, drain and set to one side.

Add the chilli flakes, spring onions, grated garlic and grated ginger to a heatproof bowl and mix well. Heat the vegetable oil in a saucepan until hot, then carefully pour over the spice mixture (the oil will partially cook your ingredients) and mix again. Now add the light soy sauce, dark soy sauce, peanut butter, mirin and crushed peanuts. Mix well.

Place the cooked noodles and beansprouts in a bowl, pour over the sauce and combine, transfer to serving bowls and tuck in.

SPICY MINCED PORK FRIED RICE

Serves 2

Preparation time: 10 minutes

Cooking time: 8 minutes

2 tbsp vegetable oil

Bunch of spring onions (scallions), cut into 3cm (1¼in) lengths

1 red (bell) pepper, cut into strips

2–3 garlic cloves, roughly chopped

250g (9oz) minced (ground) pork

Pinch of salt and white pepper

1 x 250g (9oz) packet of microwave or pre-cooked long-grain or basmati rice

150g (5½oz) beansprouts

For the sauce

3 tbsp sriracha

2 tbsp light soy sauce

1 tsp sugar

3 tbsp water

Many East Asian cuisines have their variant of chilli sauce. Sriracha, best known for its use in Thai food, is commonly available and lends its bold flavours to this dish. Tender minced (ground) pork, vibrant spring onions (scallions) and crisp vegetables dance in a zesty sriracha-infused sauce, delivering a satisfying stir-fried bowl of deliciousness.

Combine all the sauce ingredients in a bowl and set to one side.

Heat a wok over a medium-high heat, add the oil and fry the spring onions and red pepper for 2–3 minutes until charred. Add the garlic and cook until fragrant. Now add the pork and stir-fry for 3 minutes, or until the meat has browned. Add the salt and white pepper and mix well. Now add the rice, combine well and once warmed, add the sauce and continue to fry until all the ingredients are combined and heated all the way through. Finally, add the beansprouts, stir through and cook for a further minute. Once everything is fully combined and piping hot, transfer to serving plates and enjoy.

MINCED LAMB AND AUBERGINE NOODLES

Serves 2

Preparation time: 15 minutes

Cooking time: 10 minutes

85g (2¾oz) diced aubergine (eggplant)

1 tsp salt

2 nests of udon noodles

1 tbsp vegetable oil

450g (1lb) minced (ground) lamb (20% fat)

2 spring onions (scallions), finely chopped

1 tbsp minced garlic

½ tbsp minced ginger

3 red chillies, finely chopped

For the sauce

1 tbsp light soy sauce

1 tbsp oyster sauce

1 tsp dark soy sauce

½ tsp Chinese five spice

½ tsp dried chilli flakes

2 tsp chicken powder

1 tsp sugar

2 tsp cornflour (cornstarch)

2 tbsp water

Satiate your taste buds with the rich and spicy flavours of my lamb and aubergine (eggplant) noodles. This quick and satisfying stir-fry combines succulent lamb, tender aubergines and aromatic spices, all served on a bed of plump udon noodles.

Place the diced aubergine on a plate and sprinkle over the salt, then massage the salt into the aubergine and allow it to sit for 10 minutes. This will draw out any excess water. After 10 minutes, squeeze the aubergine gently and discard any excess water.

Rehydrate the noodles following the instructions on the packet. In most cases this means placing the noodles in a bowl and pouring over boiling water, then once the noodles have separated and softened, drain. Arrange in serving bowls.

Combine all the sauce ingredients in a bowl and mix well.

Place a wok over a medium heat, add the oil and, once hot, fry the lamb until browned. Then add the spring onions, garlic and ginger. Fry until fragrant and then add the drained aubergine. Stir-fry for another minute or two, then add the red chillies and give everything a good mix. Give the sauce mixture a stir to loosen the cornflour that will have settled at the bottom and add to the wok, then stir and gently bring to the boil. Once piping hot, spoon the spicy lamb over the noodles and enjoy hot.

RED CHILLI PASTE GLASS NOODLES

Serves 2

Preparation time: 10 minutes

Cooking time: 5 minutes

100g (3½oz) glass noodles

150g (5½oz) beansprouts

60g (2¼oz) carrots, peeled and cut into thin matchsticks

80g (2¾oz) cucumber, cut into thin matchsticks

For the sauce

3 tbsp gochujang

1 tbsp gochugaru

2 tbsp rice vinegar

1 tbsp sugar

2 tbsp water

2 tbsp fish sauce

2 garlic cloves, minced

1 tbsp sesame oil

1 tbsp toasted sesame seeds

Chinese cuisine frequently incorporates chilli bean paste (doubanjiang) and Sichuan pepper in its dishes for depth and heat. The dynamic layering of flavours – spicy, tangy and umami – is a method cherished across East Asia for its capacity to transform a simple noodle dish into a complex and satisfying meal. These noodles take inspiration from Korean flavours, being bathed in a spicy, tangy sauce featuring gochujang paste and Korean chilli powder, then tossed with crisp beansprouts, carrots and cucumber. An explosion of texture and flavour in every bite!

Place the glass noodles in a bowl and cover with boiling water. After 2 minutes, drain and set the noodles to one side.

Place the beansprouts, carrots and cucumber into another bowl and pour over boiling water. Steep for 2 minutes, then drain.

Mix all the sauce ingredients together, except the sesame seeds, and stir thoroughly ensuring the sugar is dissolved. Now add the noodles and drained vegetables. Mix well, ensuring all the ingredients are covered in the sauce. Transfer to serving bowls and sprinkle with the sesame seeds to serve.

GARLIC TOMATO QUICK NOODLES

Serves 1

Preparation time: 10 minutes

Cooking time: 5 minutes

250g (9oz) ready-to-wok noodles (use your favourite)

For the sauce

2 tbsp finely chopped garlic

3 spring onions (scallions), finely chopped (whites and greens separated)

2 tbsp tomato purée (paste)

1 tsp dried chilli flakes

½ tsp chilli powder of your choice

2 tbsp vegetable oil

1 tbsp light soy sauce

2 tsp Chinese black vinegar (or you can use rice vinegar)

Indulge in the tantalizing flavours of these luscious, flavour-packed noodles that can be prepared in just 15 minutes, making it the perfect choice for a quick and satisfying meal. This recipe serves one, ideal for solo lunches or quick dinners.

Place the ready-to-wok noodles in a bowl and cover with boiling water. Once the noodles have softened and separated, drain and set to one side.

In a large heatproof bowl, add the garlic, spring onion whites, tomato purée, chilli flakes and chilli powder and mix well. In a small saucepan, heat the oil and, once hot, carefully pour over the sauce mixture while stirring. Now add the soy sauce and vinegar, mix well and toss in the loosened noodles. Combine and transfer to a serving bowl. Top with the spring onion greens and tuck in.

STIR-FRY NOODLES

Serves 1–2

Preparation time: 5 minutes

Cooking time: 10 minutes

- 1 nest of egg noodles
- 1 tbsp vegetable oil
- 3 garlic cloves, minced
- 200g (7oz) boneless, skinless chicken thighs, thinly sliced
- 200g (7oz) chopped cabbage (I used a pointed cabbage)
- 3 spring onions (scallions), cut into 5cm (2in) lengths, bruised
- 2 tbsp kecap manis (sweet soy sauce)
- 1 tbsp sambal oelek
- 1 tbsp tomato ketchup

This is my take on mie goreng, a Chinese Indonesian dish featuring kecap manis, a thicker, sweeter version of sweet soy sauce that's heavily used throughout Indonesia. Noodles were likely introduced to Indonesia centuries ago by Chinese migrants, then adapted to suit local ingredients and tastes while maintaining a strong Chinese influence. In fact, the word mie comes from the Chinese word for noodle!

If your noodles are dried, begin by hydrating them in boiling water (following the instructions on the packet). Ensure the noodles are well drained and dried before stir-frying them. If preferred, you can use ready-to-wok noodles which are already soft.

Place a wok over a medium-high heat, add the oil and garlic and, once fragrant, add the sliced chicken. Once the chicken begins to brown, then add the cabbage. Stir-fry for 1–2 minutes, then add the softened noodles and spring onions and continue to fry for a further minute. Next, add the kecap manis, sambal oelek and tomato ketchup. Reduce the heat to medium and continue to cook until the ingredients are well combined and heated all the way through.

A full-flavour dish that needs no accompaniment.

HOMEMADE CHEESY TTEOKBOKKI

Serves 2

Preparation time: 8 minutes

Cooking time: 10 minutes

12 sheets of rice paper

12 cheese strips (use your favourite brand)

3 tbsp gochujang

½ tbsp garlic purée

1 tbsp light soy sauce

½ tbsp fish sauce

1 tbsp sugar

350ml (1½ cups) water

1 tbsp chicken powder

1 small onion, cut into strips

Bunch of spring onions (scallions), cut into 5cm (2in) lengths

Korean cuisine uses gochuchang in a similar way to how Chinese cuisine employs doubanjiang to employ a deep, spicy flavour. These moreish rice paper rolls are stuffed with gooey cheese then simmered in a delicious sauce, creating a harmonious blend of sweet, savoury and spicy. Perfect for sharing!

Take one sheet of rice paper and immerse it in warm water for 10 seconds, then place it on to a work surface. Place a cheese strip roughly a quarter of the way up the rice paper, which should now be pliable. Fold the end of rice paper nearest to you over the cheese strip, creating a cylinder. Then fold in the sides to seal in the cheese and continue to roll until you have a cylinder. Repeat until you have 12 cheese rolls. Now, using a pair of scissors, cut each roll in half.

Add the remaining ingredients to a saucepan or wok over a medium heat and, once it begins to boil, pop in the rice paper rolls and cook for 2–3 minutes.

Transfer to serving bowls and savour the gooey goodness.

GOLDEN EGG-GLAZED RICE BOWL

This quick and easy dish features crispy fried eggs, stir-fried with cooked white rice, and a unique sauce made from cola, soy sauce and oyster sauce. Finish it off with a generous sprinkle of chopped spring onions (scallions) for a heartily satisfying meal.

Serves 2

Preparation time: 2 minutes

Cooking time: 15 minutes

- 5 eggs
- 3 tbsp vegetable oil
- 200ml (scant 1 cup) cola
- ½ tbsp light soy sauce
- ½ tbsp dark soy sauce
- 1 tbsp oyster sauce
- 350–400g (2 cups) cooked white long-grain rice
- 5 spring onions (scallions), finely chopped (greens and whites separated)

Crack the eggs into a bowl.

Place a wok over a high heat, then add the oil and, once hot, add the eggs but do not stir them, as you want whole, crispy fried eggs. Once the eggs are crispy on one side, flip them over and cook until crispy and cooked all the way through. Reduce the heat if they are cooking too quickly.

Remove the cooked eggs and cut them into bite-sized pieces, then place half of the chopped eggs back into the wok over a medium-high heat, along with the cola, light and dark soy and oyster sauce. Cook for 3 minutes, or until the liquid has begun to reduce by a third. Now add the cooked rice and mix well, then add the spring onion whites and stir. Continue to cook until the rice is piping hot. Switch off the heat, then add the remaining cooked eggs and fold them through the rice. Transfer to serving bowls and top with the spring onion greens.

SESAME CHILLI NOODLES

Serves 2

Preparation time: 5 minutes

Cooking time: 25 minutes

- 2 tbsp tahini
- 1 tbsp light soy sauce
- 1 tbsp fish sauce
- 1 tbsp minced garlic
- 1 tbsp sugar
- 2 nests of fresh egg noodles (use your favourite ready-to-wok noodles)
- 1–2 tsp Chinese chilli oil (or use your favourite chilli sauce)
- 1 tbsp toasted sesame seeds
- 2 spring onions (scallions), finely chopped

Indulge in the delectable allure of fresh egg noodles bathed in a tantalizing blend of tahini, soy sauce and fiery chilli oil, crowned with toasted sesame seeds and spring onions (scallions).

Begin by mixing together the tahini, soy sauce, fish sauce, garlic and sugar in a medium heatproof bowl.

Bring a saucepan or wok of water to the boil and cook the noodles. If you are using the fresh egg noodles, these only take 1 minute in boiling water. Drain and set the noodles to one side, reserving 120ml (½ cup) of the noodle water.

Add the noodle water to the sauce and stir well, then add the cooked noodles and gently mix so each strand is covered in the sauce.

Transfer the noodles to serving bowls, then top with the chilli oil, sesame seeds and spring onions.

BLACK PEPPER PRAWN UDON

Serves 2

Preparation time: 5 minutes

Cooking time: 8 minutes

For the noodles

2 nests of ready-to-wok udon noodles (or your favourite ready-to-wok noodles)

1 tbsp vegetable oil

1 tbsp minced garlic

300g (10½oz) raw king prawns (jumbo shrimp), peeled and deveined

250g (9oz) pak choi (bok choy), cut into bite-sized pieces

For the sauce

2 tbsp oyster sauce

1 tbsp light soy sauce

½ tbsp dark soy sauce

1 tbsp Chinese black vinegar

½ tbsp sesame oil

1 tbsp ground black pepper

1 tbsp cornflour (cornstarch)

120ml (½ cup) water

2 tsp chicken powder

Indulge in a quick, easy to prepare, yet irresistible blend of flavours with this combination of succulent king prawns (jumbo shrimp), tender pak choi (bok choy) and udon noodles in a rich black pepper sauce. In just a few minutes, you'll have a restaurant-worthy meal to enjoy at home. Savour the bold, aromatic essence of Chinese cuisine tonight!

Begin by mixing all the sauce ingredients together.

Place the ready-to-wok udon noodles in a bowl and cover with boiling water. Once loosened, drain and set to one side.

Place a wok over a medium heat, add the oil and garlic and fry until fragrant. Now add the king prawns and cook for 1–2 minutes. Then add the noodles, fry for a further minute and pour over the sauce. Increase the heat to medium-high and, once the sauce and noodles are fully combined, add the pak choi. Cook for a minute, then transfer to serving bowls and enjoy.

SOFT, CRISPY EGG RICE NOODLES

Serves 2

Preparation time: 10 minutes

Cooking time: 12 minutes

2 nests of dried thin rice noodles (or use your favourite thickness)

3 tbsp vegetable oil

2 eggs

3 garlic cloves, minced

2 Thai red chillies, finely chopped

4 hot dogs (franks), cut into bite-sized pieces

1.2 litres (5 cups) boiling water

2 tbsp chicken powder

1½ tbsp light soy sauce

1 tsp dark soy sauce

1 tbsp sugar

¼ tsp white pepper

70g (2½oz) shredded Chinese leaf (Napa cabbage)

180g (6oz) beansprouts

3 spring onions (scallions), finely chopped

Salt, to taste

A comforting dish that combines textures and flavours in a symphony of taste. Discover the art of achieving perfectly crispy eggs, balanced with the subtle heat of Thai chillies and the crunch of fresh beansprouts.

Place the rice noodles into a bowl and cover with boiling water to rehydrate. Once softened, drain and set to one side.

Heat a wok over a high heat and, once smoking, add the oil. Now add one egg and fry until crispy on both sides. Remove to a holding plate and repeat with the remaining egg. Once the second egg is crispy on both sides, return the first cooked egg to the wok, along with the garlic and chopped chillies, and fry until fragrant. Now add the hot dog pieces followed by the boiling water. Then add the chicken powder, light and dark soy sauces, sugar and white pepper. Add the rehydrated noodles and Chinese leaf and bring to the boil. Once the soup is boiling, add the beansprouts then stir, check for seasoning and add salt if required. Finally, divide between two bowls, top each one with a soft, crispy fried egg and garnish with the chopped spring onions.

SPICY PEANUT NOODLES

Serves 2

Preparation time: 5 minutes

Cooking time: 5 minutes

2 nests of Chinese dried flat noodles (use sliced or hand-cut noodles if you can)

3 spring onions (scallions), finely chopped

For the sauce

3 tbsp crunchy peanut butter

1½ tbsp Chinese chilli oil

3 tbsp light soy sauce

2 tsp dark soy sauce

2 tsp sesame oil

1 tbsp garlic paste

3 tsp rice vinegar

3 tbsp just-boiled water

2 tbsp honey

These quick and easy-to-make noodles are coated in a creamy blend of crunchy peanut butter, Chinese chilli oil and soy sauce, creating a spicy, savoury and utterly satisfying dish. Perfect for a speedy lunch or cosy supper.

Cook the noodles following the packet instructions, then drain.

Combine all the sauce ingredients in a bowl. Once the noodles are cooked and drained, add them to the sauce and combine well. Transfer to serving bowls and top with the chopped spring onions.

PORKY YAKI UDON

Serves 2–4

Preparation time: 5 minutes

Cooking time: 12 minutes

- 2 nests of udon noodles
- 2 tbsp vegetable oil
- 250g (9oz) thinly sliced pork loin
- 3 garlic cloves, minced
- 1 onion, thinly sliced
- 3 spring onions (scallions), thinly chopped into 5cm (2in) strips (whites and greens separated)

For the sauce

- 2 tbsp oyster sauce
- 1 tbsp light soy sauce
- 2 tsp dark soy sauce
- 1 tbsp mirin
- 1 tbsp brown sugar
- 1 tbsp rice vinegar

Discover the savoury delight of porky yaki udon – thinly sliced pork loin, crisp spring onions (scallions) and tender udon noodles dance in a flavourful symphony of oyster and soy sauces.

Soften the noodles in boiling water, drain and then set to one side.

In a separate bowl, mix all the sauce ingredients together.

Heat a wok over a medium-high heat, add the oil and, once hot, add the thinly sliced pork. Once the pork begins to brown, add the garlic, followed the onion and spring onion whites. When the onion has softened, add the drained udon noodles. Reduce the heat to medium, then pour over the sauce and gently bring all of the ingredients together. Once piping hot, transfer to serving bowls and top with the spring onion greens.

Chef's Tip

To get really thin slices of pork loin, place the pork in the freezer for 20–30 minutes then, once it is partially frozen, carefully slice into very thin bite-sized slices.

VIETNAMESE-INSPIRED EGG ROLLS

Serves 6

Preparation time: 15 minutes

Cooking time: 6 minutes

18–20 spring roll wrappers

2 tsp plain (all-purpose) flour, mixed with a little water to make a paste

Vegetable oil, for frying

Lettuce of your choice, to serve

Dipping sauce of your choice, to serve

For the filling

65g (2½oz) black fungus (wood ear mushrooms), finely chopped

2 nests of glass noodles (mung bean noodles)

250g (9oz) raw king prawns (jumbo shrimp), peeled, deveined and minced

300g (10½oz) minced (ground) chicken

125g (4½oz) peeled and finely diced carrot

125g (4½oz) finely diced onion

2 tbsp minced garlic

1 tbsp minced ginger

1 tbsp chicken powder

1 tbsp sugar

Pinch of salt

2 tbsp fish sauce

These egg rolls are a mouthwatering combination of minced (ground) prawns (shrimp), chicken and delicate spices, encased in crispy wrappers. Vietnamese egg rolls traditionally feature glass noodles and a rice paper casing, but here I've used Chinese spring roll wrappers as they are easier to find in supermarkets. These tasty rolls are quick to make and perfect for dipping in your favourite sauce, creating a savoury treat for everyone at the table.

When you buy black fungus from a Chinese supermarket it will be dried. Place the dried fungus in a bowl, pour over boiling water and allow to rehydrate for 2–3 minutes. Once rehydrated, drain and set to one side (it should weigh about 155g/5½oz). The black fungus expands a lot, so don't feel you need to increase the quantity when it's in its dried state, unless you like lots!

In a separate bowl, add the glass noodles and pour in boiling water. Leave for 3 minutes, drain and allow to dry a little. Once dried, chop into small pieces.

Now place all the filling ingredients in a large bowl and mix well.

Separate the spring roll wrappers, take one sheet and place 2 tablespoons of the filling into the wrapper. Carefully roll into a cylinder and, just before you get to the end, use the flour paste to help seal the edge of the wrapper. This will prevent it from bursting open during frying. Repeat until all the filling and wrappers have been used.

In a deep-sided saucepan, heat 7.5–10cm (3–4in) of oil to about 180°C (350°F). Add the egg rolls in batches and fry until golden brown and cooked all the way through. This will take around 6 minutes for each batch. Remove the cooked egg rolls from the pan and allow to drain and cool slightly before serving.

To serve, take a lettuce leaf, place an egg roll in the centre and wrap the leaf around the roll. Dip in your favourite sauce and enjoy.

TRIPLE DELIGHT SPICY FRIED RICE

Serves 2

Preparation time: 5 minutes

Cooking time: 7 minutes

2 tbsp vegetable oil

2 eggs, beaten

100g (3½oz) diced Spam

65g (2¼oz) diced chicken breast

110g (3¾oz) small prawns (shrimp), cooked and peeled

250–300g (9–10½oz) cooked rice (or you can use 1 x 250g (9oz) packet of pre-cooked or microwave long-grain rice)

3 spring onions (scallions), finely chopped (whites and greens separated)

2 tbsp doubanjiang

1 tbsp tomato ketchup

Salt and white pepper, to taste

This quick and satisfying dish brings together the unmistakeable savouriness of diced Spam, chicken and prawns (shrimp) with a fiery kick of chilli bean paste.

Place a wok over a medium-high heat, add the oil and, once smoking, add the beaten eggs. After a few seconds – when the eggs are nearly cooked – add the Spam, chicken and prawns. Toss to combine and cook for 1 minute, then add the cooked rice and spring onion whites. Fry until the rice is toasted and heated all the way through. Add the doubanjiang and tomato ketchup, mix well and then check the seasoning. Taste and adjust with salt and white pepper to your liking. Finally, toss in the spring onion greens, mix, and serve in simple bowls with spoons for a perfect relaxed feed.

SWEET SOY SPRING ONION NOODLES WITH CRISPY CHICKEN

Serves 2

Preparation time: 5 minutes

Cooking time: 15 minutes

2 nests of noodles (use your favourite – dried or ready-to-wok)

250g (9oz) or 4 skin-on, boneless, chicken thighs

Pinch of salt

Pinch of ground black pepper

1 tbsp vegetable oil

Bunch of spring onions (scallions), cut into 5cm- (2in-) thin strips

2 garlic cloves, minced

1 tbsp toasted sesame seeds

For the sauce

3 tbsp kecap manis (sweet soy sauce)

1 tbsp mirin

1 tsp chicken powder

2 tsp sesame oil

120ml (½ cup) water

Tender chicken atop springy noodles, adorned with aromatic toasted sesame seeds. A delicate sensory explosion in every mouthful!

If you are using dried noodles, rehydrate them following the packet instructions, then drain and set to one side.

Mix together all the sauce ingredients.

Season the chicken thighs with the salt and pepper. Place a wok over a medium-high heat, add the oil and the seasoned chicken, skin-side down. Once the skin has browned, turn the chicken over and cook until browned and cooked all the way through. Remove the chicken from the pan and allow it to rest while you cook the noodles.

Return the wok, with the residual oil and chicken fat, to the heat and add the spring onions. Once the spring onions begin to char, add the garlic and fry until fragrant. Now stir in the noodles and after a minute add the sauce, continuing to cook until heated through. Transfer the saucy noodles to serving bowls, slice the cooked chicken into bite-sized pieces and place on top of the noodles, then finally sprinkle with toasted sesame seeds and enjoy.

CREAMY CURRY UDON NOODLES

Serves 2

Preparation time: 5 minutes

Cooking time: 6 minutes

2 tbsp vegetable oil

4 garlic cloves, roughly chopped

200g (7oz) mushrooms, sliced (use your favourite)

300ml (1¼ cups + 1 tbsp) single (light) cream

50g (1¾oz) Japanese or katsu curry paste

2 nests of ready-to-wok udon noodles

2 spring onions (scallions), finely chopped

While curry isn't traditionally Chinese, the curries of neighbouring countries have been adapted into Chinese cuisine and takeaway-style cooking. In a nod to the origins of the sweet, mild Chinese curries you may be familiar with, this Japanese-inspired dish is quick to prepare, uniting plump udon noodles with a rich Japanese curry paste, mushrooms and cream. A delightful fusion of flavours awaits.

Place a wok over a medium heat, add the oil and fry the garlic until it is golden brown but not burnt. Now add the mushrooms and cook until tender. Pour in the cream and curry paste and keep stirring until the paste has dissolved and the sauce is heated through. Add the noodles, mix well, and once the noodles are hot, transfer to serving bowls. Top with the chopped spring onions to serve.

EASY BOILED RICE

Serves 4

Preparation time: 5 minutes

Cooking time: 25 minutes

400g (2 cups) long-grain rice

This method is a foolproof way to create perfect boiled rice every time. To make life even easier, I'd recommend buying a rice cooker. It really is an invaluable piece of kitchen equipment that I wouldn't be without!

In a medium saucepan or rice cooker, add the rice and fill with warm water. Rubbing your hands together, wash the rice, then carefully drain the water. Repeat at least three times, as this process removes some of the starch.

Cover the washed rice with water so it sits 2.5cm (1in) above the rice. If using the traditional finger dip method, the water should come up to your first knuckle. Turn the heat on to high and boil – it is important you do NOT stir. You must pay FULL ATTENTION to the pan now. Once the water has been absorbed and tiny craters appear in the rice, reduce the heat to its lowest setting and place the lid firmly on to the saucepan (sealing in the steam). Leave for 3 minutes and then switch off the heat – it is very important you do NOT remove the lid (no peeking). Leave the rice to steam in the residual heat for a further 10 minutes.

Remove the lid and stir the rice with a spoon to loosen the grains. You should have perfect fluffy rice ready to serve immediately.

If you are using a rice cooker, once you have covered the rice with water simply pop on the lid and turn it on. The rice cooker will do the job perfectly from there on.

sweet things and drinks

STEAMED BAO BUNS

Makes 6

Preparation time: 1 hour 15 minutes

Cooking time: 9 minutes

120ml (½ cup) warm full-fat milk

10g (¼oz) caster (superfine) sugar

5g (⅛oz) dried yeast

200g (1½ cups) plain (all-purpose) flour

5g (⅛oz) baking powder (baking soda)

1½ tsp olive oil

For a sweet filling (optional)
Lotus seed paste, custard or red bean paste

For the pork filling (optional)

80g (3oz) Cantonese roast pork

½ tbsp sugar

1 tbsp hoisin sauce

1 tbsp yellow bean sauce

1 tsp Chinese five spice

2–3 tbsp water

natural red food colouring

½ tbsp vegetable oil

According to Ming Dynasty scholars, the original name for these buns, mantou, meant 'barbarian's head'! These steamed, soft white buns are traditionally served with tea.

Add the milk to a jug along with the sugar and yeast. Stir and leave to ferment for 5 minutes. In a large bowl, combine the flour and baking powder, make a well in the centre, then pour in the yeast mixture and mix thoroughly to form a dough. Knead for 5 minutes. Lightly rub ½ teaspoon of olive oil over the surface of the dough and leave in the bowl, covered with a damp cloth or cling film (plastic wrap) to prove for 30 minutes, until doubled in size.

If making the pork filling, chop the pork into 5mm (¼in) cubes. Mix the remaining ingredients (except the oil) in a bowl and set aside. Heat the oil in a wok and fry the pork for 30 seconds. Add the sauce mixture and stir vigorously for 2–3 minutes. Tip the filling back into the bowl and leave to cool.

Turn out the dough on to a floured work surface and knead out any air bubbles, keeping your work surface dusted with flour. Using your hands, roll the dough into a long sausage, then divide into 6 equal pieces. Form each piece into a 7cm (2¾in) flat disc. You can leave them unfilled, or add a tablespoon of the pork filling or your filling of choice into the centre of each disc and gather up the edges to form a round parcel, twisting the top to form a seal.

Place the filled dough balls onto perforated baking parchment in a bamboo steamer with a lid, cover with a damp cloth and leave to prove again for 30 minutes.

To cook, place the bamboo steamer over a pan of boiling water and steam the buns for 9 minutes. Serve hot.

BANANA FRITTERS

Serves 4

Preparation time: 10 minutes

Cooking time: 15 minutes

- Groundnut oil for deep-frying
- 260g (2 cups) self-raising (self-rising) flour
- ½ tsp bicarbonate of soda
- 360ml (1½ cups) water
- 4 bananas, peeled and halved
- 130g (1 cup) plain (all-purpose) flour

To serve

- 6 tbsp golden syrup
- 4 scoops vanilla ice cream

Gooey bananas covered in a fluffy batter and served with a blob of ice cream and oozing golden syrup. Yum!

We often ate this at the end of 'staff dinner' as the head chef had a sweet tooth, and while he was cooking the bananas he'd leave the tin of golden syrup in a bowl of warm water to make it extra runny for drizzling over the top.

Heat enough oil in a wok or deep-sided saucepan so you can deep-fry the bananas, to 170°C (340°F).

Sift the self-raising flour into a large bowl, add the bicarbonate of soda and the water and mix to form a smooth batter. Lightly dust the bananas in plain flour, then dip into the batter to coat and carefully drop into the oil. Deep-fry for around 6–8 minutes, until golden brown. Transfer to a wire rack or a plate lined with paper towels to drain.

Divide between four plates, drizzle over the golden syrup and add a scoop of ice cream to serve.

SWEET PEANUT MOCHI

Serves 4

Preparation time: 5 minutes

Cooking time: 5 minutes

For the peanut coating
160g (1 cup) salted peanuts
2 tbsp sugar
Pinch of fine salt

For the mochi
175g (1 cup) glutinous rice flour
240ml (1 cup) water
1 tbsp sugar
Pinch of salt
Vegetable oil, for greasing

These chewy, glutinous rice cakes are filled with luscious, sweet peanuts, serving up a perfect blend of sweetness and nutty richness in every bite. These 'can' serve four if you're prepared to share!

Place the peanuts into a blender and, using the pulse setting, blend until you have a peanut powder. Do this slowly as the peanuts get hot and will want to turn into butter. Empty the powder into a bowl and combine with the sugar and salt.

Now add all the mochi ingredients to a heatproof bowl and mix well, cover loosely with cling film (plastic wrap) and microwave on high for 3 minutes. Then, using a wet spoon, give the mixture a stir, cover again and microwave for another minute.

Lightly grease your hands and a spoon with oil, take 1 heaped tablespoon of mochi mixture and then dump into the peanut powder. Shape into a cylinder, rolling it in the powder to cover. Repeat until all the mochi mixture has been used – you should have about 8 balls. Enjoy!

ICED COFFEE TEA

Serves 4

Preparation time: 2 minutes

Cooking time: 3 minutes

4 teabags

1 x 397g (14oz) tin (can) sweetened condensed milk

480ml (2 cups) strong coffee

Strange as it sounds, this drink complements lots of savoury dishes. I use instant coffee and it tastes just fine but feel free to use your favourite filter blend!

Boil 1 litre (4 cups) of water in a saucepan and add the teabags. Simmer over a medium heat for 3 minutes, then squeeze out and discard the teabags. Remove from the heat, stir in the condensed milk until fully dissolved, then add the coffee. Stir well and pour into 4 glasses filled with ice. Serve.

INDEX

THANK YOU

At the heart of every endeavour, personal or professional, there lies a force that propels us forward, nudging us towards our dreams and cushioning our falls. For me, that force has been Jo Wan, my beloved wife.

Jo, words often fall short when I attempt to encapsulate the gratitude, love and appreciation I feel for you. Your unwavering support, your boundless love and your enduring faith in me have been the bedrock upon which I've built my dreams. It was your encouragement that allowed me to transform my knowledge for cooking into a tangible reality, allowing me to pen my culinary adventures and share them with the world.

Through the trials and tribulations, the successes and missteps, you've been my anchor. Your belief in me, even during moments when I doubted myself, has been the wind beneath my wings. You've celebrated my successes, offered solace during setbacks and provided a listening ear during moments of introspection.

This book, like every dish I've ever created, carries a piece of my heart. But equally, it's a testament to your love and faith. It is as much yours as it is mine.

To Jo, for being my confidante, my partner in crime, my muse and my pillar of strength: thank you. Here's to the love that simmers, the dreams that sizzle and the journey that we continue to embark upon, hand in hand.

I'll follow you to the farthest reaches of space, my darling!

ABOUT THE AUTHOR

Kwoklyn Wan is a professional chef, restaurateur and Kung Fu instructor. Kwoklyn is the brother of television celebrity Gok Wan, and the two brothers grew up working in their family's Cantonese restaurant in the Midlands, UK. This is his seventh book.

Quadrille, Penguin Random House UK, One Embassy Gardens, 8 Viaduct Gardens, London SW11 7BW

Quadrille Publishing Limited is part of the Penguin Random House group of companies whose addresses can be found at global.penguinrandomhouse.com

Penguin Random House UK

Published by Quadrille in 2025
www.penguin.co.uk

A CIP catalogue record for this book is available from the British Library

ISBN 978 1 78713 910 7
10 9 8 7 6 5 4 3 2 1

Managing Director Sarah Lavelle
Copy Editor Vicky Orchard
Art Direction and Design Katherine Case
Cover Illustration Jordan Amy Lee
Photographer Sam Folan
Food Stylist Katie Marshall
Prop Stylist Agathe Gits
Head of Production Stephen Lang
Senior Production Controller Martina Georgieva

Colour reproduction by F1

Printed in China by C&C Offset Printing Co., Ltd.

The authorised representative in the EEA is Penguin Random House Ireland, Morrison Chambers, 32 Nassau Street, Dublin D02 YH68.

Penguin Random House is committed to a sustainable future for our business, our readers and our planet. This book is made from Forest Stewardship Council® certified paper.

MIX
Paper | Supporting responsible forestry
FSC® C018179